A YEAR OF

Pies

A YEAR OF

Pies

A Seasonal Tour of Home Baked Pies

ASHLEY ENGLISH

LARK
Asheville

Senior Editor
NICOLE MCCONVILLE

Editor
BETH SWEET

Creative Director
CHRIS BRYANT

Art Director
TRAVIS MEDFORD

Photographer
LYNNE HARTY

Cover Designer
TRAVIS MEDFORD

LARK

An Imprint of Sterling Publishing
387 Park Avenue South
New York, NY 10016

If you have questions or comments about
this book, please visit: larkcrafts.com

Library of Congress Cataloging-in-Publication Data

English, Ashley, 1976-
  A year of pies : a seasonal tour of home baked pies / Ashley English.
       p. cm.
  Includes index.
  ISBN 978-1-4547-0286-3 (pbk. : alk. paper)
  1. Pies. I. Title.
  TX773.E545 2012
  641.86'52--dc23
                                        2012003261
10 9 8 7 6 5 4 3 2

Published by Lark Crafts
An Imprint of Sterling Publishing Co., Inc.
387 Park Avenue South, New York, NY 10016

Text © 2012, Ashley English
Photography © 2012, Lark Crafts, an Imprint of Sterling Publishing Co., Inc.,
unless otherwise specified
Illustrations © 2012, Lark Crafts, an Imprint of Sterling Publishing Co., Inc.,
unless otherwise specified

Distributed in Canada by Sterling Publishing,
c/o Canadian Manda Group, 165 Dufferin Street
Toronto, Ontario, Canada M6K 3H6

Distributed in the United Kingdom by GMC Distribution Services,
Castle Place, 166 High Street, Lewes, East Sussex, England BN7 1XU

Distributed in Australia by Capricorn Link (Australia) Pty Ltd.,
P.O. Box 704, Windsor, NSW 2756 Australia

ISBN 13: 978-1-4547-0286-3

For information about custom editions, special sales, and premium and corporate purchases, please
contact Sterling Special Sales Department at 800-805-5489 or specialsales@sterlingpub.com.

Requests for information about desk and examination copies available to college and university
professors must be submitted to academic@larkbooks.com. Our complete policy can be found at
www.larkcrafts.com.

CONTENTS

WINTER

SPRING

INTRODUCTION

AYear Of Pies is crafted exactly as I cook, directly parallel with the seasons as they manifest here in the Northern Hemisphere. In the heat of summer, you'll catch me selecting the juiciest, ripest, most transcendently fragrant tomatoes I can gather, either from my local market or my home garden, and rendering them, along with a bit of basil and eggplant, into an otherworldly Ratatouille and Polenta Pie (page 127). You won't, however, find me turning out my Strawberry Crumble Pie (page 69) in December or assembling my Cranberry Mince Tart (page 157) in July, as tempting as they may be. Not only is it easier to find ingredients that are readily available with the seasons, they taste a million times better! So why bake any other way?

From the frost of winter on through the dog days of summer, this book presents recipes that are informed by the best of what is available year-round. Robust, hearty savory pies and bright, sweet citrus offerings when the mercury dips give way to light, refreshing, fruit-filled pies and straight-from-the-garden options for lunch or dinner when the heat is on. At the start of each seasonal chapter, you'll find a listing of fruits and vegetables that ripen during that stretch of months. The recipes will then feature many of those items in pies that will satisfy your sweet tooth and tame your growling tummy. There are tried-and-true classics (everyone needs a Classic Blueberry Pie, page 123, come summertime), along with many modern takes on much-loved favorites (my Limoncello Lemon Meringue Pie, page 39, will leave you wondering why you haven't always made it this way).

I also include a short history of pie—a rather fascinating tale from its humble origins as an inedible vessel in which to hold foods to its current place in the pantheon of culinary staples. You'll find a "hand-holding" chapter on all-things related to Crusts, where I guide you through the entire process, from mixing it up, to rolling it out, to making it lovely. There are chapters that detail the Equipment and Ingredients I've found to make the most exquisite pies imaginable, as well. Sprinkled throughout, you'll discover bits of my pie-baking wisdom—little slivers of advice I've learned along my journey that'll make an expert pie baker out of you, too. Lastly, but certainly far from least, I present you with recipes from a number of my pie-making friends (all bloggers), who have graciously shared some of their most delectable creations, both sweet and savory alike.

Creating a delicious pie emboldens you while it satiates you. It lifts you up and gives you hope. I know that sounds grandiose (it's only humble pie, after all, right?), but it's true. Crafting and baking pie is an exercise in patience with a reward in contentment. You need to do things just so (and in this book I'll take your hand and guide you through exactly what "just so" entails). You must measure with precision. You must chill the dough (several times) sufficiently. But never mind all of that, dear pie-maker. The finished product, you see, is so delicious, so lovely, so lauded by those who consume it that the mindful steps taken to reach that end point make it all incredibly worthwhile.

Many folks shy away from pie, thinking it's much too finicky or persnickety for them. Having spent time as a professional baker, I can tell you with the utmost confidence that baking pie is considerably easier than baking many, many other things. Sure, you've got to follow the recipe and handle the dough with love and care. Sure, it's a bit more time consuming than opening up a premixed box of cake, stirring in a few ingredients, and popping the batter in the oven. But, the taste of homemade pie packed with ripe fruit, veggies, or meat and baked into flaky, sweet submission is without comparison.

My goal with this book is to inspire, excite, and embolden you to begin creating fresh, ripe, seasonally delicious pies yourself. Although I baked my first pie years ago, around age eight, I still become excited and optimistic every time I bring out the rolling pin and open up the flour canister. Hope manages to spring eternal each time I line the pie pan and fish the pastry cutter out of the utensil drawer. Although the pies I bake now are a bit more polished than my first, their crusts a bit flakier, their edges a bit less browned, the start-to-finish process is just as engaging, just as gratifying as it was so long ago. I lift my rolling pin in salute and wish you an epic pie adventure.

Ashley English

A HISTORY OF PIE

LIKE ANY GOOD BIT of culinary lore, the history of pie is long and storied, not to mention a bit murky. A number of debates exist surrounding the specifics, and the further back one goes, the more the definition of a pie is stretched. Many consider pie's roots to reach all the way to ancient Egypt, when those wise, intrepid pyramid builders used to drip honey onto pounded grains and bake the concoction over an open fire. Later, bakers to the pharaohs were known to have baked honey, fruits, and nuts into bread dough in a sort of primitive, early incarnation.

The Greeks, who probably picked up their pie inspiration from the Egyptians, are credited with making the first stuffed pastry, which was used to seal and store foods but may not have been eaten itself. A little more than a thousand years ago, the Romans took the tradition from the Greeks and expanded on it with the spices and culinary knowledge that came with their conquests. In turn, their pie tradition spread throughout the vast Roman empire, adapted to local food sources and customs.

This is probably what the British tradition of pie (originally "pye") stems from. Many believe that the term, which appeared early in the 1300s, is an abbreviation of "magpie," referring to a bird known for its appetite for all sorts of different foods. Pies of the time similarly incorporated a mix of a number of different ingredients, including meats and fruits.

During medieval times, there were two types of pie: sealed pastry pies that were known as "coffins" (a reference to their boxlike shape), and versions with an open top that were called "traps." The crusts of these pies were hard and most likely not intended to be eaten, although edible crusts did become more popular toward the end of the era. Most of the pies during that time were meat- and sauce-based, not the fresh produce pies that are more common today.

When the Pilgrims arrived in America in 1620, they brought the concept of pie with them. Venison and other wild game were common fillings, which also included fruits and berries—pointed out to the Pilgrims, it is claimed, by Native Americans. Some say it was the Pilgrims who invented the round pie as a way to literally cut corners, as ingredients needed for making pastry crusts were scarce. The early Pilgrims still used the medieval term "coffin" for their pies.

As the eighteenth-century Age of Enlightenment rolled around, pies began to more closely resemble the modern incarnation. Cookbooks with recipes came into being. The pies they offered became more refined, and the pastry was now often edible. Some of the earliest recognizable versions of pies that we now enjoy made their appearance, among them apple pie—which, despite its association with America, originally came from England (apologies to Johnny Appleseed!). Savory pies were the most common version in America until the twentieth century, and while they continue to be the order of the day in Europe, dessert pies are most popular in the States today.

Clearly, when it comes to pie and its history down through the ages, the pastry-cloaked dish is beloved the globe over, a fact on which we can all—happily and heartily—agree!

PIE-MAKING BASICS

TOOLS

Several tools are necessary to successfully create pies and tarts. While some are indispensable, others merely make the task at hand considerably easier. You may very well already have a number of these items in your kitchen. Remember, pie making has been practiced for generations, with great results coming out of kitchens both humble and grandiose. Gather up a pan wsor two and a rolling pin, partner them with your own capable hands, and watch all manner of delicious pies and tarts stream out of your oven!

COOKIE AND PASTRY CUTTERS

These tools are helpful in several ways. Cookie cutters are useful for cutting out disks of dough when making hand pies. I use a set of circular cutters in increasing sizes for this very purpose. Pastry cutters allow for artful decoration of double-crust pies, which require some sort of steam ventilation. It's also possible to vent pies with pie birds (see page 13) or by making simple slits with a knife. Pastry cutters can also be used for a decorative edge, such as overlapping leaves or triangles, in single-crust pies.

PARCHMENT PAPER

This nonstick, heat-resistant paper is great for lining piecrusts that will be blind baked (see page 30). Simply tear off a square of parchment that is just slightly larger than the pie's circumference, place it atop the crust, line the crust with pie weights or dried beans, and you're ready to bake!

FOOD PROCESSOR

A food processor can be used to cut butter and shortening into flour. Using the "pulse" button, simply chop the fats into the flour in short bursts. You want to be sure to leave some larger globules of fat in, as they're what's responsible for flakiness. With my food processor, all that's needed to pulse in the fats properly is about 5 to 6 bursts. Then water, just enough for the dough to start to come together, is added in stages. Your objective is for the dough to begin to clump together just enough to be formed into large balls by hand. You don't want it mounding up around the blade inside the processor itself.

PIE PANS

Most pie pans will get the job done just fine. There are pros and cons to every kind, so I suggest experimenting a bit to see what kind you like working with.

Glass: The most ubiquitous is the trusty glass pie plate. It browns well, cooks evenly, and allows you to get a look at how the crust is doing as it bakes. Many have handles, which allow you to grip the plate without breaking the crust. Glass pie plates are typically available in two main sizes: a standard 9-inch and a deep dish, which holds more filling. This book has recipes for both sizes. Glass pie plates can be found in just about any supermarket or kitchen store, and are usually quite inexpensive.

Ceramic: Ceramic dishes are often the prettiest pie pans available to the home baker. These dishes cook similar to glass; both styles conduct heat more slowly than metal, which helps when you want the filling to set before the crust browns. A good ceramic pie plate is as equally beautiful for serving as it is for baking in. Although they tend to cost considerably more than other options, I'd argue that it's worth it to splurge for one you truly like. We appreciate food with our eyes as well as our mouths, after all.

Cast iron: I find that cast-iron pie pans cook similar to ceramic pie pans. They're also quite attractive, producing a pie possessing an "old-fashioned" appeal. Cast-iron pie pans often have handles, as well, which is a big plus in my book.

Metal: Metal pans are usually a lighter weight than the other options, and are durable and trustworthy for the most part. Metal pans can be subdivided into two categories: dark metal or light metal (referring to the color of the pan itself). Darker metal pans conduct heat more quickly, so the crust crisps faster—handy for no-bake pies. Lighter metal pans slow the baking process down somewhat, which is helpful when you want to be sure that the filling has set before the crust browns too much.

Aluminum foil: The standard, lightweight, disposable aluminum-foil pans that most store-bought pies come in are very convenient and super lightweight, but they can be wobbly and tend not to crisp the crust quite as well.

PASTRY BLENDER

If you intend to make piecrusts by hand (as opposed to using a food processor), then a pastry blender will be indispensable. A U-shaped tool with a series of curved, horizontally-positioned blades or wires located opposite the handle, a pastry cutter allows you to cut in butter and shortening with ease. You can also substitute two knives for a pastry blender if you prefer, although I find that the handle and multiple blades on this device allow you to cut in the fats much more quickly.

PASTRY BRUSH

This tool is handy for brushing an egg wash on top of your piecrust, which gives it a golden sheen once baked. I use a pastry brush made of silicone bristles. I find it much easier to clean than a brush fashioned from animal bristles, which often sheds.

PIE BIRD

Also known as a pie vent, funnel, or chimney, this hollow ceramic tool is used to vent rising steam from pies. While less commonly used in modern baking, pie birds were frequently employed in Victorian era ovens, which routinely suffered from problems of uniform heating. The birds permitted the escape of steam, thus preventing a pie's contents from boiling over. Pie birds do have their place in the pie world of today, however. Serving as a functional bit of ornamentation, they imbue pies with whimsy and nostalgia.

PASTRY WHEEL

A pastry wheel is helpful in creating a lattice-top piecrust. Either a straight-edge or a fluted wheel will enable you to cut strips with ease. I use a sewing measuring tape as a measurement guide, which helps to cut strips of equal length and width.

PIE MARKER

Also referred to as a "pie cutter" or "slice marker," this tool enables you to cut slices of equal size simultaneously. Available as 6-, 7-, 8-, 10-, and 12-slice cutters, pie markers are incredibly helpful when you want to cut a set number of equally proportioned slices.

PIE SERVER

A handled wedge-shaped tool, pie servers are used in removing slices of pie from pans. Some have a serrated edge on one side to use in cutting gently into a pie's crust. There are also pie server models that are incorporated into the pie pan before the crust is added. The pie is baked with these servers in place, allowing you to lift the first pie slice from the pan without marring the rest of the pie.

PIE SHIELD

A pie shield serves two functions. It helps the pie to rise in the middle, thus preventing spillage. Also, by keeping the crust edge covered, it protects it from burning. Pie shields are available in silicone or aluminum, as either 9-inch circles or small, curved pieces. They are reusable.

PIE WEIGHTS

Made from ceramic or metal beads, pie weights help to weigh down an empty piecrust that is being prebaked. Without weight added to it, an empty crust would both puff up and shrink during cooking. Pie weights offer counterweight, preventing this from occurring. Dried beans can also be used in lieu of pie weights, an economical substitute that can be used again and again, and stored in a jar. If you opt for the beans route, be sure to cool them thoroughly after removing them from your piecrust before returning them to their jar. Oh, and handle with care—they'll be hot!

Whatever medium you choose, be sure to fill the empty crust with weights all the way up to its rim prior to baking. I found this out the hard way when my heretofore gorgeous piecrust shrank down to one-quarter its original size, post bake.

ROLLING PIN

A sturdy rolling pin is essential for flattening dough into piecrust. Several models are available to the home baker, with the "best" style ultimately being whatever feels the most comfortable to you. Personally, I prefer either a 12-inch wooden pin with wooden handles, or a similarly sized pin with a non-stick surface and contoured handles for easy grip. Other bakers like the coolness and weight of a marble rolling pin, while many also like the straightforwardness and tactile nature of a tapered wooden dowel with no handles, referred to as a "French" rolling pin. I encourage you to visit a baking supply store and test out a number of the styles available. What might be ideal for one baker won't be the first choice for another.

SCISSORS

A pair of kitchen shears is helpful for trimming overhanging pie dough—much easier and more manageable than attempting to do the job with a knife. Scissors will also come in handy when cutting parchment paper.

SILICONE BAKING MAT

This reusable, pliant baking mat can be used in place of parchment paper. Placed underneath a disk of dough, the mat keeps the rolled-out dough from sticking to countertops. It can also be used to line a baking sheet, to collect drips or overflow that may occur during baking. Aside from their use in pie and tart-baking, silicone baking mats are immensely helpful in baking cookies, scones, or any other baked goods that would otherwise be directly on a baking sheet.

SPRINGFORM PANS

A springform pan is a type of bakeware with removable sides, and the word "springform" refers to how the pan works. The pan's flat, circular base separates from its ring-shaped sides, which makes it ideal for baking dishes that can't be easily inverted or removed from the pan. A latch on the exterior of the sides clamps shut to tighten the ring to the pan's base, securing them together when the pan is in use. When the latch is unclamped, the sides spring open.

TART PANS

Tart pans have fluted edges and are available in both circular and rectangular styles. These pans are made with removable bottoms, which support the tart and save the tarts' decorative edges when you remove them from the pan. Tart pans are made of either tin or nonstick material.

INGREDIENTS

To build a great pie, you need great ingredients. You wouldn't choose sad wilted flowers and expect to create a gorgeous bouquet. Similarly, starting out with quality ingredients provides an ideal foundation for crafting an expert, and delicious, pie. Here I've provided notes on some of the ingredients called for in this book. The specific items I use in my kitchen were selected after a good deal of trial and error. Use my tips, spare yourself the snafus I experienced when experimenting with ingredients, and end up with nothing but forkfuls of exquisite pie!

BUTTER

For pie-making, I use unsalted butter. I like controlling the amount of salt in my piecrusts, and include a small amount of it, along with flour, water, and sometimes shortening (depending on whether I'm making an all-butter or a butter/shortening crust) when I'm mixing up pie dough. As such, I find salted butter to be unnecessary. When using butter for pie dough-making purposes, be sure it's straight-from-the-fridge cold. It's essential that butter be cold for it to flake up properly once baked into a piecrust. I store sticks of butter in my freezer, transferring them to my refrigerator to thaw out the night before making a piecrust.

CHOCOLATE

When chocolate is called for in this book, you'll want to use a dark variety, which includes semisweet and bittersweet. Personally, I like my chocolate as dark and bitter as possible. If you prefer a slightly sweeter offering, however, then choose a variety with a lower cacao percentage (this information is typically available on the label). The higher the percentage, the more bitter the chocolate.

TIP When making any baked good that calls for chocolate, I like to use fair-trade labeled chocolate. Fair-trade is a social movement and system of exchange that considers all aspects of a commodity's production, including its producers, consumers, communities, and environment. Fair-trade organizations and businesses promote practices such as a living wage for employees, safe working conditions, a fair exchange rate for the goods produced, and consideration of local communities and environments. In particular, fair-trade focuses on exports from so-called "developing nations" to those in "developed" countries, and involves commodities such as handicrafts, coffee, chocolate, bananas, sugar, tea, and wine.

TIP I frequently use cultured butter in pie dough, as I find its slight tanginess makes piecrusts absolutely sublime. Cultured butter can be found in many grocery stores, as well as natural foods stores. If your local grocery doesn't carry it, refer to Resources (page 173) for an online supplier.

COOKIES

Several crusts in this book call for cookies, including chocolate wafers, gingersnaps, and graham crackers. I use pre-made, all-natural-ingredient cookies. If you lack a food processor for pulsing the cookies into fine crumbs, simply place them in a resealable bag and roll over them with a rolling pin.

MILKING THE SUBJECT

Organically produced foods are grown without the use of toxic pesticides and fertilizers. Such foods, and the animals from which they are derived, must be free of antibiotics, artificial growth hormones, genetically modified organisms (GMOs), irradiation, and sewage waste. Furthermore, the production of organic foods cannot involve the use of cloned animals, artificial ingredients, or synthetic preservatives.

Specific to dairy products, organically produced milk is certified to be free of rBGH (or rBST), a bovine growth hormone used to boost milk production in cows. Cows treated with rBGH are milked three times a day on account of the exaggerated amount of milk the hormone causes them to produce. As a result, many cows experience mastitis, an infection of the udder, and a reduced lifespan. Furthermore, the milk from rBGH-treated cows contains IGF-1, a growth hormone shared by humans and adults. There is some concern that ingestion of dietary IGF-1 via milk causes the proliferation of cancer-causing cells in humans, especially affecting reproductive organs sensitive to hormonal fluctuations.

In the United States, federally mandated standards require that third-party state or private agencies oversee organic certification for producers. The U.S. Department of Agriculture (USDA) in turn accredits these agencies. In order for a farm or dairy to become certified organic, the land and animals must not have encountered any prohibited materials for three years. Scrupulous record keeping must be on hand to prove this, in addition to a detailed plan for preventing contamination by nonorganic materials. A number of agencies around the world perform similar organic certification testing. Requirements, regulations, and oversight vary from country to country but are, for the most part, quite similar.

DAIRY

All of the dairy items used in this book—including butter, half-and-half, heavy cream, milk, and yogurt—are full-fat, or whole. I've found, in my years of baking, that full-fat products yield the best flavor and texture. I also use all organic dairy products, and often seek out those produced by small creameries, in order to support both organic agriculture and small family farms. Furthermore, I find the tastes offered by organically produced dairy products to be superior, as many organic creameries allow their cows access to grass and pasturelands, the subtle flavors of which are evident in the finished dairy items.

EGGS

All of the eggs used in this book are large size. My eggs come from my own free-range, organically fed chickens. Some recipes will require separating the egg yolks from their whites. This is easily done by cracking the egg and gently pouring the white into a bowl while passing the yolk back and forth between the two shell halves. Use chilled eggs when separating yolks from whites, as it makes separating the two easier.

For those recipes calling for room-temperature eggs, allow the eggs (still in their shells) to sit in a bowl on the kitchen counter for at least 45 minutes. Alternately, add eggs to a bowl of lukewarm water for 10 minutes. The eggs will be considered "room temperature" when they feel about the same temperature as your hand.

EXTRACTS

Whenever extracts are called for in this book, including vanilla, orange, coconut, lemon, and peppermint, you'll want to use all-natural, real extracts. Imitation extracts are not only full of synthetic flavor agents and preservatives, they lack the powerful flavor provided only by authentic extracts.

HERBS

A number of recipes call for the use of fresh herbs. I attempt to use fresh herbs, as opposed to dried, whenever possible. As the book is arranged by seasons, I've tried to make the herbs in the recipes as seasonally relevant as possible (such as basil in the summer months, but not in winter recipes). If you cannot find a source of fresh herbs, however, feel free to substitute with dried, using half the amount called for.

PRODUCE

You can only expect your finished pies, tarts, quiches, and galettes to be as good as the raw materials you begin with. As such, seek out the freshest, ripest fruits and vegetables you can find. Since this book is arranged seasonally, you'll be primed and ready to find fragrant, ripe peaches in July for a summer pie, or plump, juicy oranges in January for a winter tart. Look for bruise- and blemish-free offerings. Farmer's markets are ideal sources of fresh produce, as will be your own backyard, if you're keeping a garden. Otherwise, make friends with the produce manager wherever you shop and learn what days of the week produce deliveries are made.

FLOUR

All-purpose flour is my flour of choice when making pies and tarts. It's easy to come by, doesn't need to be sifted, and is an all-around good choice. To properly measure flour, dip your measuring cup into the bag (or container, if you're storing your flour in a canister), scoop it full, and then sweep off any excess flour with a straight-edged kitchen tool. I use a cake-frosting spatula.

TIP I keep my flour in its own bag in the freezer, along with fats like butter and shortening, so that all of the ingredients necessary for whipping up a piecrust are nice and chilled when I need them. You'll generate the flakiest piecrusts if your dough hits the oven cold, cold, cold, so keeping everything chilled along the way is one of my secrets to crust-making success!

SALT

All of the recipes in this book use finely ground sea salt. I prefer the flavor of sea salt to table salt, which I find leaves an unpleasant aftertaste (perhaps due to the inclusion of iodine in most varieties). Sea salt is readily available from most grocery stores.

SHORTENING

The Basic Pie Dough recipe in this book (page 21) can be made using butter alone, or with a blend of butter and shortening. When I use shortening, I select either an all-natural palm/soy/canola/olive oil blend or a 100 percent palm oil version, never those containing partially hydrogenated oils.

SUGARS

Unless otherwise stated, whenever sugar is called for in this book, I'm referring to granulated cane sugar. Light and dark brown sugars, when used, are specifically indicated. The difference in color between light and dark brown sugar is due to the amount of molasses each contains, with dark brown sugar containing a higher percentage. Demerara sugar is characterized by large crystals; turbinado sugar, or "raw" sugar, may be used in place of demerara. Such sugars, when called for, will supply a crunchy, sugary topping to pies.

TIP The palm shortening I use comes from sustainably managed forests and is harvested in small yields. To find a source, refer to Resources (page 173).

SPICES

Ground spices, like all foodstuffs, have a shelf life. Your pies will be more flavorful if the spices you use are fresh. Give an annual look at the expiration dates on your spice jars. Choose a date you're unlikely to forget, such as New Year's Day, or your birthday or anniversary. Anything older than a year should be composted and fresh offerings picked up. If you worry you won't go through, say, an entire bottle of ground allspice in a year, try to find a store that sells spices in bulk, purchasing only what you'll use month-to-month. Alternately, you could simply find a brand that carries smaller-sized bottles of spices.

PIECRUSTS

It can easily be argued that every great pie begins with a great crust. As the vessel containing all of the pie's contents, its flavor will be present in every forkful. Start with a great crust, and you're that much closer to ensuring pie perfection. In this chapter, we'll explore the crust recipes used in the book, tips towards baking the best crust possible, and a number of crust-related how-to's, from rolling out pie dough to forming decorative crust edges.

BASIC PIE DOUGH
(SHORTENING-AND-BUTTER VERSION)

Why use shortening in a piecrust? The general thinking is that shortening aids in creating flakiness, while butter imparts flavor. This recipe creates a crust that is just that—full of tender flakes and rich in flavor.
Makes: Dough for one double-crust pie

YOU WILL NEED

2½ cups all-purpose flour
1¼ teaspoons sea salt
  6 tablespoons (¾ stick) unsalted butter, chilled and cubed
  ¾ cup vegetable shortening, chilled and cubed
  ¾ cup ice water

Mix the flour and salt together in a medium-large bowl.

Using a pastry blender or two forks, cut in the butter and shortening until the mixture resembles coarse meal (you should still have some rather large bits of butter and shortening when you're done).

Slowly drizzle in the ice water and stir with a large spoon until the dough begins to clump.

Transfer the dough to a floured work surface and, using your hands, fold it into itself until the flour is fully incorporated into the fats. The dough should come together easily but should not feel overly sticky.

Divide the dough in half, shape it into two balls, and pat each ball into a ½-inch thick disk. Wrap each in plastic wrap (or try the alternative tip on page 22) and refrigerate for at least an hour.

Proceed according to the pie recipe instructions.

BASIC PIE DOUGH
(ALL-BUTTER VERSION)

This all-butter crust is unrivaled in terms of flavor. It's also quite flaky, despite having no shortening. The secret is to work with very cold butter. I keep all of my butter in the freezer, transferring it to the refrigerator overnight or several hours before I intend to make pie dough. Work quickly, with cold hands on a cool work surface, and you'll end up with a crust that's as flaky as it is scrumptious.
Makes: Dough for one double-crust pie

YOU WILL NEED

2½ cups all-purpose flour
1¼ teaspoons sea salt
  1 cup (2 sticks) unsalted butter, chilled and cubed
  ¾ cup ice water

Mix the flour and salt together in a medium-large bowl.

Using a pastry blender or two forks, incorporate the butter until the mixture resembles coarse meal (you should still have some rather large bits of butter and shortening when you're done).

Slowly drizzle in the ice water. Stir with a large spoon until the dough begins to clump.

Transfer the dough onto a floured work surface and, using your hands, fold it into itself until all of the flour is incorporated into the fats. The dough should come together easily but should not feel overly sticky.

Divide the dough in half, shape it into two balls, and pat each ball into a ½-inch thick disk. Wrap each in plastic wrap (or try the alternative tip on page 22) and refrigerate for at least an hour.

Proceed according to the pie recipe instructions.

GINGERSNAP CRUST

This crust is for the serious ginger lover. Big on spice and rich with butter, it's the perfect partner to my Gingersnap Key Lime Pie (page 53) and Gingersnap Pumpkin Pie with Candied Pumpkin Seeds (page 147). Although it will be soft when first removed from the oven, the crust will harden as it cools. **Makes: Crust for one 9-inch pie**

YOU WILL NEED

```
    9-inch pie pan or springform pan
10  ounces gingersnap cookies (about 2½ cups)
 6  tablespoons (¾ stick) unsalted butter, melted
```

Preheat the oven to 350°F. Lightly butter the 9-inch pie pan or springform pan and set aside.

Crush the gingersnaps either by pulsing them in a food processor or placing them in a plastic freezer bag and rolling over them with a rolling pin.

Combine the crushed gingersnaps and melted butter in a medium-size bowl. Stir until fully mixed.

Press the mixture into the pan, covering the bottom fully and pressing the crumbs halfway up the sides.

Bake the crust 10 minutes, then remove from the oven and cool completely before filling.

CHOCOLATE COOKIE CRUST

Chocolate cookie wafers or plain cookies can also be used to make this crust. While pre-made chocolate cookie crusts are readily available for purchase at grocery stores, this recipe is so easy to make, and so full of flavor, that it would be a shame to go that route. The crust will harden as it cools. **Makes: Crust for one 9-inch pie**

YOU WILL NEED

```
    9-inch springform pan
10  ounces chocolate cookie waters (about 2½ cups)
 8  tablespoons (1 stick) unsalted butter, melted
```

Preheat the oven to 350°F.

Crush the cookies either by pulsing them in a food processor or placing them in a plastic freezer bag and rolling over them with a rolling pin.

Combine the crushed cookies and melted butter in a medium-size bowl. Stir until fully mixed.

Press the mixture into the 9-inch springform pan, covering the bottom evenly and pressing the crumbs halfway up the sides.

Bake the crust 10 minutes, then remove from the oven and cool completely before filling.

TIP I'm not a big fan of disposable anything, let alone disposable plastic wrap. Whenever I make pie dough, I use a large freezer bag set inside a lidded container and sandwich the two disks of pie dough between the folded bag. Once I've used up the pie dough, I simply wash the surface of the freezer bag, leave it out to dry, and then store it away until pie baking beckons again. Easy peasy, and best of all, no waste!

ALMOND SHORTBREAD CRUST

Be sure to toast the almonds briefly before use, as doing so removes a bit of their natural moisture. To roast, bake at 275°F for 4 to 5 minutes. This also imparts a bit of smokiness in the process.
Makes: Crust for 14-inch tart or one 9½-inch round tart

YOU WILL NEED

      14-inch tart pan with removable bottom
 ¼ cup almonds, toasted
1¼ cups all-purpose flour
 ½ cup powdered sugar
 ½ teaspoon sea salt
10 tablespoons (1¼ sticks) unsalted butter, chilled
      and cubed
 1 large egg yolk

Butter the tart pan and set aside.

Place the almonds, flour, powdered sugar, and salt in a food processor. Pulse several times to fully combine, stopping before the nuts form a paste.

Add the butter to the nut mixture and pulse several times to cut in the butter until the mixture is coarse and crumbly.

Add the egg yolk and pulse several times, stopping just as the mixture begins to clump.

Press the dough across the bottom and up the sides of the prepared pan, then place the crust-lined pan in the refrigerator and chill at least 1 hour.

Preheat the oven to 375°F.

Bake the crust 15 to 20 minutes, until golden brown, then remove from the oven and cool completely before filling.

GRAHAM CRACKER CRUST

You can use either the "sheets" of prepared graham crackers or the smaller "sticks" for this recipe. Either way, be sure to begin with 8 ounces and then crush them. If making Frozen Strawberry Pie (page 71), cool the crust completely before adding the filling; otherwise it will cause the filling to melt and pool. **Makes: Crust for one 9-inch deep-dish pie**

YOU WILL NEED

     9-inch deep-dish pie plate
 8 ounces graham crackers, (about 2 cups)
 8 tablespoons (1 stick) unsalted butter, melted
 2 tablespoons granulated sugar
 ½ teaspoon sea salt

Preheat the oven to 350°F.

Crush the graham crackers either by pulsing them in a food processor or placing them in a plastic freezer bag and rolling over them with a rolling pin.

Combine the crushed graham crackers, melted butter, sugar, and salt in a medium-size bowl and stir until fully mixed.

Press the mixture into the 9-inch deep-dish pie plate, covering the bottom evenly and pressing the crumbs halfway up the sides.

Bake the crust 10 minutes, then remove from the oven and cool completely before filling.

PIE DOUGH TIPS

One of the most important things for creating a great piecrust is to keep it cool before it goes in the oven. Whether you're making an all-butter or shortening-and-butter crust, be sure that the fats are nice and cold. I even keep my flour in my freezer to have it always cool. After rolling the dough out, return it to the refrigerator to chill while you make your filling. When taking the dough out of the refrigerator to fill just prior to baking, be sure to have all of your filling and topping components ready to go. Lastly, preheat the oven so that the cold pie dough will go right into a piping hot oven for baking. Remember this phrase and you'll be in great shape: Make it cold, bake it hot.

Cut cold butter or shortening into roughly pea-size pieces before blending with the other ingredients. No need to make everything super tiny. Some scattered large bits help form flaky pockets once the dough is cooled.

Keep your hands cool, especially when adding rolled dough to the pie pan and then decoratively forming the edges. If you find you need to wash your hands when baking your pie, give them a finishing rinse under cold water at the end. Don't loose your "cool" and your pie will reward you with abundant flakiness!

Oftentimes, you'll end up with extra pie dough after rolling out your crust. You can use those leftover bits in a number of ways. Either make use of them at that time—by turning them into mini tarts, decorative crusts, or shortbread cookies—or freeze the bits for later use.

The use of pie weights is very important in blind baking (page 30). Without pie weights, the dough will shrink considerably, as well as puff up. As mentioned when discussing pie weights (page 14), fill the parchment-lined pan all the way up the sides and across the center with weights.

Ventilation is essential in double-crust pies. When baking any double-crust pie, it's imperative that you use either cutouts in the pastry dough, create several ventilation slits, or insert a pie bird (page 13). All of the moisture present inside the filling needs somewhere to go, otherwise it will pool inside the crust itself.

A golden brown crust with a bubbling filling generally equates to a finished pie. If you see a nicely browned crust and center full of bubbly goodness, chances are your pie is done.

Pre-made pie dough will last for 3 days in the refrigerator and up to 3 months in the freezer. To thaw frozen dough, simply leave it in the refrigerator overnight or for up to 8 hours.

CRUST TROUBLESHOOTING

Preventing a soggy bottom: Blind baking the crust first, to crisp it up a bit, may help with those pies that use particularly watery fillings. See page 30 for detailed instructions on blind baking. Also, you may want to check and make sure that your oven is operating at the proper temperature. An oven thermometer will let you know the temperature exactly.

Preventing a shrunken crust: Overworked pastry dough will shrink if cooked straight away, as the gluten in it has been activated. Give it time to relax a bit by cooling it in the refrigerator until you're ready to fill and bake it.

Preventing crumbly, tough pastry dough: Be sure to use adequate liquid when mixing your dough. Insufficient liquid can result in a dough that is unduly crumbly and tough.

Preventing a tough baked crust: Tough crusts are typically the result of not enough fat being included in the dough. Follow the recipes in this book just as written and you'll end up with soft, pliant, flaky piecrusts.

Preventing an overbrowned crust: To keep crust edges from getting too dark, use either a pie shield (see page 14) or a strip of aluminum foil twisted into a rope that fits the circumference of the pie pan.

MAKING BASIC PIE DOUGH

1 Using either a whisk or a fork, mix the flour and salt together in a medium-size bowl. **(A)**

2 Cut the butter into medium-small cubes. I typically cut a stick of butter lengthwise down the middle, then turn each cut stick on its side and slice it lengthwise down the middle. After that, I line up the sticks and cut about 10 slices through them, creating a number of cubes.

3 Add the cubed butter to the bowl. Using a pastry blender or two knives, work the butter (and shortening, if using) into the dough until pea-size lumps form. **(B)**

4 Add ½ cup cold water to the center of the mixture. **(C)** Using a metal spoon, stir until the water has fully moistened the dough and becomes completely incorporated. Add the remaining water in 1 tablespoon increments, just until the dough begins to form a ball.

5 Gather up the dough with your hands. Using patting movements, incorporate any remaining flour into the moistened dough. **(D)**

6 Separate the dough ball into two rounds of even size. Pat them into disks about ½ inch thick. **(E)** At this point, you can store the dough one of two ways. Either wrap both dough disks in plastic wrap, or use my method (which omits the use of plastic wrap) and place the dough disks in a lidded container with a sheet of parchment paper in between them. **(F)**

7 Chill the dough in the refrigerator for at least 1 hour before use. It can be kept for up to 3 days in a sealed container or in plastic wrap in the refrigerator. The pie dough may also be frozen for 3 months. Place frozen dough in the refrigerator overnight, to thaw.

ROLLING OUT A PIECRUST

1 You'll begin with a chilled disk of pie dough. Soften the dough, if needed, by leaving it on the counter for about 10 to 15 minutes. **(A)**

2 Sprinkle several tablespoons of chilled flour onto your countertop. **(B)**

3 Beginning in the center of the dough disk, roll it into a circle with a rolling pin. **(C)**

4 Turn the dough about a quarter turn after every few rolls. I often flip the disk over after every few rolls, to prevent it from sticking to the counter. If necessary, put down a little more flour to keep everything moving freely. **(D)**

5 Roll the dough out to ⅛-inch thickness and 12 inches in diameter (unless indicated otherwise in the recipe). **(E)**

LINING THE PIE PAN

1 Use your fingertips to gently loosen the rolled pastry dough from the countertop.

2 Roll the pastry over your rolling pin **(A)**, then lift it and rest it carefully over your pie pan of choice. **(B)**

3 Carefully tuck the pastry in across the bottom, into the edges, and up the sides of the pan. **(C)**

4 With a small pairing knife or set of kitchen shears, trim the extra overhanging bits of crust to ½ to 1 inch beyond the edge of the pie pan. **(D)**

....

TIP A swivel-style cake decorating stand is especially useful when trimming the crust overhang. It turns the entire pie pan as you go.

....

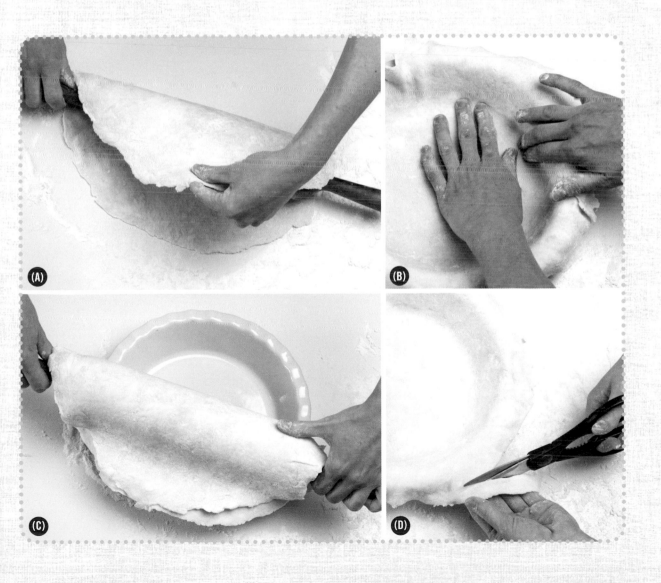

(A)

(B)

(C)

(D)

BLIND BAKING

1 You'll begin with chilled pie dough that has been rolled out and lined in a pie pan of your choice. (Be sure to pierce the bottom and sides of the chilled piecrust about 6 to 7 times, per your recipe. This process helps to keep the crust from rising and puffing up as it bakes).

2 Next, cut a square of parchment paper roughly the circumference of the pie pan. Lay the parchment atop the chilled dough. **(A)**

3 Using either pie weights or dry beans, fill the parchment-lined pie pan. **(B)** Whatever type of weights you use, be certain to fill the pan with them all the way up to the top. **(C)** Otherwise, the edges are liable to collapse or shrink during baking.

4 For a partially baked crust, bake at the temperature and duration detailed in your recipe. Remove the crust from the oven, allow it to cool 10 minutes, and then remove the weights and parchment. For a fully baked crust, after removing the weights and parchment, return the crust to the oven and continue baking for the amount of time listed in your recipe.

(A)

(B)

(C)

LATTICE

1 Using a pastry wheel (either the flat or crimped edge), cut 12 strips ½ to ¾ inches wide in the rolled pastry. If you don't have a pastry wheel, you can also use either a pizza wheel or a paring knife to cut out the strips. **(A)**

2 I use a sewing measuring tape as a guide between the strips. I've found it's the perfect length and width for the job. Lacking such a tool, you can simply cut a guide 12 inches long and ½ inch wide out of cardboard.

3 Carefully thread the strips over and under one another, pulling back strips as necessary to weave. **(B–G)**

TOPPING A DOUBLE-CRUST PIE

1 Line your pie pan with the bottom crust as indicated in Lining a Pie Pan (page 29).

2 Place your filling in the crust-lined pan. **(A)**

3 Roll out a second disk of dough as indicated in Rolling Out a Piecrust (page 28).

4 Beat together 1 large egg yolk and 1 tablespoon of cold water, creating an egg wash. Brush the top edge of the bottom crust with the egg wash.

5 Lift the top crust onto a rolling pin and center it evenly as you lay it over the pie pan. **(B)**

6 Trim the overhanging top crust to 1 inch. **(C)**

7 Fold the top overhang under the bottom crust overhang. Press together with your fingers, creating a seal. **(D)**

8 Choose the piecrust edge motif of your choice (page 34) and create accordingly. **(E)**

9 Using a small pairing knife, cut several ventilation slits in the top crust. **(F)**

10 Brush the top of the crust with the remaining egg wash and bake according to the recipe. **(G)**

CREATING DECORATIVE PIECRUST EDGES

While it's entirely possible to make a delectable pie without ornamenting its crust, doing so helps convey the inherent specialness of what's in store. The following five decorative crust treatments are easy to master and transform a pie from "humdrum" to "wow" in minutes.

FLUTED

1 Bend the index and middle finger on your writing hand.

2 Place the two fingers against the outer crust edge.

3 Use the knuckle of the index finger on the opposite hand to push against the inside of the crust edge, forming indentations.

4 Repeat around the entire circumference of the crust.

FORK CRIMP

1 Dip the tines of a fork in cold flour.

2 Press the tines into the crust edge all the way around.

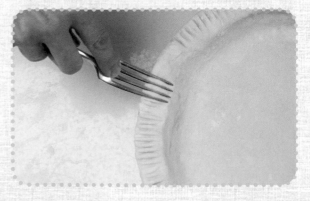

HERRINGBONE

1 Dip the tines of a fork in cold flour.

2 Press the tines into the crust edge, alternating the direction of the tines for every indentation.

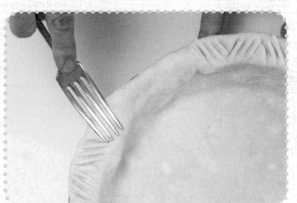

CUTOUT

1 Use ½- to ¾-inch cookie or pastry cutters to cut about 20 to 25 shapes out of rolled-out dough.

2 Brush the top of the crust edge with cold water.

3 Arrange the dough cutouts in an overlapping pattern around the entire edge.

WINTER

Ah, winter. Icicles, snowflakes, and short days are what might immediately come to mind when one thinks of the season. It might surprise you, then, to realize that an abundance of produce, literally ripe for pie making, is at its peak in winter. While a number of items continue to grow all winter long, others come into season and taste their finest during the days of mittens and woolens. I've included chocolate in the mix, too. Although not a "seasonal" item in the truest sense of the term, it certainly has its place in the lineup, as its pick-me-up properties make it a much-loved gray-day staple.

BEETS * CABBAGE * CELERIAC

CITRUS FRUITS (including: blood oranges, clementines, kumquats, lemons, limes, Meyer lemons, oranges, and tangerines)

COLLARDS * KALE * MUSHROOMS

ONIONS * PARSNIPS * POTATOES

RUTABAGAS * TURNIPS

LIMONCELLO LEMON MERINGUE PIE

If you like a tart lemon pie, then this puckery version is for you. Ample quantities of lemon juice and zest, combined with a healthy dose of the Italian liqueur Limoncello, create a pie that's just as pleasing to taste as it is to smell. Perfect for a winter doldrums pick-me-up, promising the return to hot, sunny days with every bite. *Makes: One 9-inch pie*

YOU WILL NEED

- ½ recipe Basic Pie Dough (page 21)
- 9-inch pie pan

FILLING

- 1 cup water
- 1 cup granulated sugar
- ⅓ cup cornstarch
- ¼ teaspoon sea salt
- 5 large egg yolks
- ⅔ cup lemon juice
- ⅓ cup Limoncello
- Grated zest of two lemons
- 4 tablespoons (½ stick) unsalted butter, cubed

MERINGUE

- 3 large egg whites, at room temperature
- 1 teaspoon vanilla extract
- ¼ teaspoon cream of tartar
- 6 tablespoons granulated sugar

Preheat the oven to 400°F.

 TIP Allowing the egg whites to come to room temperature first will better ensure your achieving a fluffy, pillowy meringue.

VARIATION: Don't want the booze? Simply omit the Limoncello and increase the water to 1⅓ cups.

PREPARE THE CRUST

Roll out the dough on a lightly floured surface and fit into the 9-inch pie pan. Trim the crust overhang to 1 inch and crimp the edges decoratively. Prick the bottom of the crust 6 or 7 times with a fork, then place the crust in the refrigerator for 15 minutes.

Line the crust with parchment paper and fill with dried beans or pie weights. Bake 12 to 15 minutes, then remove from the oven, leaving the oven on.

Remove the dried beans or pie weights and parchment paper from the crust, and return it to the oven. Bake an additional 5 to 7 minutes, until the crust is golden.

Cool completely before filling.

PREPARE THE FILLING

Combine the water, sugar, cornstarch and salt in a medium-size saucepan. Whisk until fully blended and bring to a boil over medium-high heat. Whisking constantly, cook for 3 minutes. Turn the heat to low.

Remove ½ cup of the cooked mixture and pour it slowly over the egg yolks in a small bowl, whisking constantly until well combined.

It's essential that you take your time when adding the cooked mixture to the eggs, otherwise they'll curdle. Pour it in a gentle, steady stream, whisking vigorously the entire time.

Return the egg yolk mixture to the saucepan on the stove. Whisk in the lemon juice, Limoncello, lemon zest, and butter. Beat until the butter is melted and the mixture is fully combined.

Remove the pot from the heat and pour the filling into the prebaked crust.

PREPARE THE MERINGUE

Using an electric mixer or a whisk, beat the egg whites with the vanilla and cream of tartar until soft peaks form. Gradually add the sugar, one tablespoon at a time, and beat until stiff peaks form.

ASSEMBLE THE PIE

Pile the meringue over the filling, mounding it in the center and covering the filling completely. Make sure you touch the edges of the crust all around, to prevent the meringue from shrinking.

Using the lowest broiler setting of your oven, evenly brown the meringue topping for about 1 minute. Or, if you have one, use a handheld culinary blowtorch.

Place the pie in the refrigerator and keep chilled until ready to serve.

ORANGE CURD TART WITH ALMOND CRUST

If you've got a wintertime brunch, shower, or luncheon to host, this tart will be the dessert you'll want to offer your guests. The slight crunch of the crust is the perfect foil to the curd's creaminess. A sprinkle of confettied candied orange peel on top adds a festive note.

Makes: One 14-inch tart. A 9½-inch round tart pan can also be used.

YOU WILL NEED

Almond Shortbread Crust (page 23)

CANDIED ORANGE PEEL

1   orange

¾   cup granulated sugar

½   cup water

CURD

4   large eggs

1¼ cups granulated sugar

10 tablespoons (1¼ sticks) unsalted butter

Juice and grated zest of 4 oranges

VARIATION: Walnuts, pecans, or hazelnuts will also work equally well in the crust here. Simply substitute an equal amount of the toasted nut of your choice for the almonds.

PREPARE THE CANDIED ORANGE PEEL

Line a baking sheet with parchment or waxed paper. Set aside.

Cut the top and bottom off the orange. Make 4 scoring indentations through the peel around the remaining orange. Pull off the peel sections and set the fruit aside for another use. Scrape out the pith with a spoon and discard, then cut each section of peel into ¼-inch strips.

Bring a small saucepan filled with water to a boil. Add the strips and boil for 1 minute, then drain in a colander and rinse under cold water. Repeat this process two more times.

Return the empty saucepan to the stove and add the sugar and water. Stir over medium-high heat until the sugar dissolves.

Turn the heat to high and bring the mixture to a boil. Add the orange strips, reduce the heat to low, and simmer until soft and translucent, about 15 to 20 minutes.

Using tongs, remove the peel from the saucepan and spread on the reserved lined baking sheet. Leave to dry at room temperature for at least 1 hour. Once dry, chop up the strips of peel into small (¼ inch) pieces.

PREPARE THE CURD

Place the eggs in a medium-size metal or glass bowl. (Do not use a plastic bowl, as you'll be placing it atop of saucepan of simmering water.) Beat well, incorporating the whites into the yolks.

Fill a medium-size saucepan with about 2 inches of water and place over medium-high heat. Bring to a gentle simmer. Reduce heat to low.

Put the metal or glass bowl with the eggs on top of the saucepan, forming a double boiler. Add the sugar, butter, orange juice, and zest; whisk gently until the sugar dissolves and the butter melts.

Stir the mixture with a wooden or metal spoon until it thickens and coats the back of the spoon, about 15 to 20 minutes.

Remove the curd from the heat, transfer to a lidded container, and refrigerate until cool.

ASSEMBLE THE TART

Fill the prepared crust with the chilled curd and spread with a rubber spatula to distribute evenly. Sprinkle the candied orange peel on top. Keep the tart refrigerated until ready to serve, removing the sides of the tart pan before serving.

CHOCOLATE, COFFEE, AND ORANGE MARMALADE TART

Transforming oranges into marmalade is a smart way of making the most of this fruit when it's at the peak of ripeness. The addition of fresh vanilla bean creates a marmalade reminiscent of orange Creamsicles. Chocolate and orange have a long and storied history of playing off one another's flavors, and they do so expertly here. This being a rich tart, small wedges are all that's needed to satisfy a cold evening's sweet tooth. *Makes: One 9-inch tart*

YOU WILL NEED

Chocolate Cookie Crust (page 22)

Muslin tea bag

MARMALADE

1 pound oranges

1½ cups water

½ vanilla bean

1 cup granulated sugar

1 tablespoon lemon juice

GANACHE

1 cup heavy cream

11 ounces bittersweet chocolate (preferably one with at least 60 percent cocoa content), chopped

3 tablespoons strong coffee or coffee-flavored liqueur such as Kahlúa

TIP Save the vanilla bean casing once you've scraped out the seeds. Add it to a canister of granulated sugar for a delicious infused sugar—perfect for baking, adding to tea, or gifting to loved ones.

PREPARE THE MARMALADE

Quarter the oranges. Once quartered, separate the peel from the flesh. Scrape out the pith with a spoon and discard.

Chop the flesh into small pieces, removing seeds as you see them. Place the seeds in a muslin tea bag (they contain a good deal of pectin and will aid in thickening the marmalade).

Slice the peel into long thin strips, and then cut the strips into smaller, ½-inch pieces.

Put the seed bag, fruit flesh, sliced peel, and water in a large, heavy stainless-steel soup pot or stockpot. Bring to a boil over medium-high heat. Boil for 5 minutes, then cover and remove from the heat. Allow to cool at room temperature overnight or for at least 8 hours.

Remove the lid from the pot and place the pot over medium-high heat. Bring the mixture to a gentle simmer, then reduce the heat to low and cook 10 minutes.

Slice the vanilla bean open and use the tip of a paring knife, scrape out the seeds inside. Add the seeds to the pot.

Add the sugar and lemon juice. Stir to fully combine, then cook uncovered over low heat for 25 minutes, until the mixture begins to thicken. Remove from heat and set aside.

PREPARE THE GANACHE

Place 1 to 2 inches of water in a medium-size saucepan and turn on the heat to high. Put a metal bowl over the saucepan, creating a double boiler. Combine the heavy cream and chocolate in the bowl. As the water begins to boil, the chocolate will start to melt. Whisk the mixture every few minutes, until the chocolate has melted and is thoroughly blended with the cream. Whisk the coffee or liqueur in with the melted chocolate.

Remove the bowl from over the saucepan and set aside.

ASSEMBLE THE TART

Spread the marmalade evenly across the surface of the cookie crust. Pour the ganache over the marmalade, using a spatula to smooth the surface if necessary.

Refrigerate until firm; this should take between 1 to 2 hours.

BUTTERED RUM SHOOFLY PIE

A staple of Pennsylvania Dutch cooking, shoofly pie developed as much out of need as desire. Early settlers to the area brought pantry staples that could weather the long boat ride, including flour, brown sugar, molasses, lard, salt, and spices. Arriving in late autumn, the settlers had to wait until the following spring to obtain fresh produce. Longtime fans of pies, they gave birth to shoofly, using those nonperishable items brought with them from home. While the origin of the pie's name is still a matter of culinary world debate, the most widely held belief is that it derived from swarming flies that gathered over the pools of molasses, formed while the pies baked in large, outdoor ovens. Packed with spices redolent of winter, shoofly pie is best served warm, and with a bit of whipped cream. *Makes: One 9-inch pie*

YOU WILL NEED

- ½ recipe Basic Pie Dough (page 21)
- 9-inch pie pan

FILLING

- 1 cup all-purpose flour
- 1 cup (packed) light brown sugar
- ½ cup (packed) dark brown sugar
- 1 teaspoon ground allspice
- 1 teaspoon ground cinnamon
- 1 teaspoon ground nutmeg
- ½ teaspoon ground cloves
- ½ teaspoon sea salt
- 8 tablespoons (1 stick) unsalted butter, cubed
- ¾ cup water
- ¼ cup dark rum
- 1 teaspoon baking soda
- ½ cup blackstrap molasses
- 3 large eggs, beaten
- Whipped cream or vanilla ice cream, to serve

Preheat the oven to 375°F.

PREPARE THE CRUST

Roll out the dough on a lightly floured surface and fit it into the 9-inch pie pan. Trim the crust overhang to 1 inch and crimp the edges decoratively. Place in the refrigerator.

PREPARE THE FILLING

Mix together the flour, sugars, spices, and salt in a large bowl. Using a pastry blender or two forks, cut in the butter until pea-size crumbs form.

Bring the water and rum to a boil in a medium-size saucepan over high heat. Remove from the heat and pour the mixture into a medium-size bowl. Whisk in the baking soda and molasses.

Add the eggs, beating well to combine, then stir in a little more than half of the prepared crumb mixture.

ASSEMBLE THE PIE

Pour the molasses mixture into the chilled piecrust and sprinkle with the remaining crumble topping. Set the pie pan on a rimmed baking sheet and bake 45 minutes, or until the filling is set.

Cool at least 1 hour before serving with whipped cream or vanilla ice cream.

VARIATION: If you'd like this without alcohol, omit the rum and substitute 2 teaspoons rum extract or vanilla extract.

BRANDY AND SPICE APPLE HAND PIES

A hand pie is one of the most fun means of consuming pie, in my opinion. It's eminently portable, making it ideal for munching during wintertime activities like ice skating, sledding, or simply warming up around a fire ring. It also makes clean-up a cinch, as there's no need for a plate or fork. Here, apples are paired with warming winter spices, including cardamom, one of my favorites. The brandy adds a bit of warmth and draws out the fruitiness of the apples. *Makes: Eight hand pies*

YOU WILL NEED

- ½ recipe Basic Pie Dough (page 21)
- 4-inch circular cookie cutter
- 2 baking sheets lined with parchment paper or a silicone mat

FILLING

- 4 tablespoons (½ stick) unsalted butter
- 2 pounds apples (such as Gala, Granny Smith, Jonagold, or a blend of baking apples), peeled, cored, and cut into ¼-inch thick slices
- 2 tablespoons lemon juice
- ⅓ cup brandy
- ¼ cup (packed) light brown sugar
- 1 teaspoon sea salt
- ½ teaspoon ground cinnamon
- ½ teaspoon ground nutmeg
- ½ teaspoon ground cardamom
- ¼ teaspoon ground cloves
- 2 tablespoons all-purpose flour
- ¼ cup dried currants

EGG WASH

- 1 large egg yolk
- 1 tablespoon whole milk

CINNAMON SUGAR

- ¼ cup granulated sugar
- 1 tablespoon ground cinnamon

PREPARE THE HAND PIECRUSTS

Remove the chilled pie dough from the refrigerator and roll it out into a 12 to14-inch circle on a lightly floured surface. Cut out sixteen 4-inch rounds using a circular cookie cutter. Re-roll scraps as necessary.

Transfer the dough rounds to the lined baking sheets, placing 8 disks on each sheet, and refrigerate while you prepare the filling.

PREPARE THE FILLING

Melt the butter in a skillet over medium low heat. Add the apples and sauté for about 8 minutes, stirring frequently.

Stir in the lemon juice, brandy, sugar, salt, and spices and cook for about 10 minutes, or until the apples are limp and fragrant.

Stir in the flour and currants; cook 2 to 3 minutes, until the apples have absorbed the flour and the liquid has cooked off.

ASSEMBLE THE HAND PIES

Preheat the oven to 350°F.

Remove the baking sheets of chilled dough rounds from the refrigerator.

On one baking sheet, mound 2 to 3 tablespoons of apple mixture on top of each dough round, leaving about a ¼-inch border.

Place the remaining dough rounds on top of each pie and press the edges with the tines of a fork to seal.

Beat the egg yolk with the milk in one small bowl. In another bowl, stir the sugar with the cinnamon to mix thoroughly.

Brush the egg wash lightly over the top of each pie with a pastry brush, then sprinkle each with several teaspoons of cinnamon sugar.

Bake for 25 to 30 minutes, until the crusts are golden brown. Cool at least 30 minutes before serving.

VARIATION: If you'd prefer not to use brandy, simply replace it with an equal amount of apple juice.

LEMON-LIME CHESS PIE

Mainstays of classic Southern cooking, chess pies contain a filling of eggs, sugar, butter, and a bit of flour. Some variations (including this one) include cornmeal, while others add a bit of vinegar. Why the word "chess" is applied is uncertain. A number of theories abound, including one asserting the term referred to the pie "chest" or cabinet used to cool these sugary pies. This offering combines lemon and lime juice and zest, creating a tangy filling with just a hint of crunch, courtesy of the cornmeal. *Makes: One 9-inch pie*

YOU WILL NEED

½ recipe Basic Pie Dough (page 21)

9-inch pie pan

FILLING

1¾ cups granulated sugar

3 tablespoons cornmeal

½ teaspoon sea salt

4 large eggs, beaten

4 tablespoons (½ stick) unsalted butter or margarine, melted

¼ cup lemon juice

¼ cup lime juice

2 tablespoons grated lemon zest

2 tablespoons grated lime zest

Preheat the oven to 350°F.

PREPARE THE CRUST

Roll out the dough on a lightly floured surface and fit it into the 9-inch pie pan. Trim the crust overhang to 1 inch and crimp the edges decoratively. Place in the refrigerator.

PREPARE THE FILLING

In a large bowl, combine the sugar, cornmeal, and salt; stir with a fork to fully mix. Add the remaining ingredients and whisk until completed blended.

ASSEMBLE THE PIE

Pour the filling into the chilled crust. Set the pie pan on a rimmed baking sheet and bake 40 to 45 minutes, or until the filling is firm around the edges (don't worry if the center is a bit jiggly—it'll firm up once it cools).

Cool completely before serving.

MINTY CHOCOLATE CREAM PIE

Chocolate has a long history of heavy wintertime consumption. From hot chocolate beverages sipped with Christmas cookies, to boxes filled with Valentine's truffles, chocolate and a dip in the mercury go hand in hand. Perhaps it's all the mood-elevating properties chocolate contains that make it such a desirable indulgence when branches are barren and the sky is gray. This pie capitalizes on the happy marriage of chocolate and mint. A robust chocolate pudding is crowned with a minty whipped topping, guaranteed to chase away the blues. *Makes: One 9-inch pie*

YOU WILL NEED

½ recipe Basic Pie Dough (page 21)

9-inch pie pan

FILLING

2½ ounces sweetened baking chocolate, chopped

¾ cup granulated sugar

3 tablespoons cornstarch

½ teaspoon sea salt

2 cups whole milk

3 large egg yolks, beaten

3 tablespoons unsalted butter

2 teaspoons vanilla extract

WHIPPED TOPPING

2 cups heavy cream

2 tablespoons powdered sugar

1 teaspoon peppermint extract

Chocolate shavings or crushed peppermint candies, to serve (optional)

Preheat the oven to 400°F.

PREPARE THE CRUST

Roll out the dough on a lightly floured surface and fit it into the 9-inch pie pan. Trim the crust overhang to 1 inch and crimp the edges decoratively. Prick the bottom of crust 6 or 7 times with a fork, then place the crust in the refrigerator for 15 minutes.

Line the crust with parchment paper and fill with dried beans or pie weights. Bake 12 to 15 minutes, then remove from the oven, leaving the oven on.

Remove the dried beans or pie weights and parchment paper from the crust, and return it to the oven. Bake an additional 5 to 7 minutes, until the crust is golden.

Cool completely before filling

PREPARE THE FILLING

Combine the chocolate, sugar, cornstarch, and salt in a medium-size saucepan. Add the milk and bring to a boil. Cook 2 minutes, stirring constantly, then turn the heat to low.

Remove ½ cup of the cooked mixture and pour it slowly over the beaten egg yolks in a small bowl, whisking constantly until thoroughly combined.

It's essential that you take your time when adding the cooked mixture to the eggs, otherwise they'll curdle. Pour it in a gentle, steady stream, whisking vigorously the entire time.

Return the egg yolk mixture to the saucepan on the stove. Cook over medium-low heat for 2 to 3 minutes, whisking constantly.

Remove from the heat and whisk in the butter and vanilla until the butter is melted and the mixture is smooth. Pour into the prebaked crust.

PREPARE THE WHIPPED TOPPING

Using whisk or a mixer on high speed, beat the heavy cream, powdered sugar, and peppermint extract until billowy peaks form.

ASSEMBLE THE PIE

Pile the whipped topping over the pie, mounding it in the center and covering the filling completely. Sprinkle chocolate shavings or crushed candies over the top, if using.

Place in the refrigerator and keep chilled until ready to serve.

GINGERSNAP KEY LIME PIE

A gingersnap crust, instead of the customary graham cracker offering, is my update on this classic pie. My recipe is inspired by time spent baking ginger lime cookies at an Asheville, North Carolina, bakery while a freshman in college. The heat of ginger is a natural complement to the tartness of Key limes. A native of the Florida Keys, these limes are smaller and thinner-skinned than their cousin the Persian lime. If you cannot find them fresh, bottled juice works equally well.

Makes: One 9-inch pie

YOU WILL NEED

Gingersnap Crust (page 22)

FILLING

¼ cup key lime juice

3 tablespoons grated lime zest

1 can (14 ounces) sweetened condensed milk

3 large egg yolks, beaten

Preheat the oven to 350°F.

PREPARE THE FILLING

Combine the lime juice, lime zest, sweetened condensed milk, and eggs in a medium-size bowl. Whisk until ingredients are fully blended.

ASSEMBLE THE PIE

Pour the filling into the prepared cooled crust and bake 15 minutes.

Cool completely before serving.

TIP To extract as much juice as possible from the tiny limes, roll them on their sides over a hard surface with the palm of your hand. Doing so breaks up the membranes inside, making the juice more readily available.

MAPLE ORANGE WALNUT PIE

Harvested and boiled into sweet perfection in late winter/early spring, maple syrup heralds the return to longer days and warmer weather. Coupled with oranges and walnuts, this pie delivers on texture, aroma, and flavor. A dollop of whipped cream is entirely optional, but heavily recommended. *Makes: One 9-inch pie*

YOU WILL NEED

- ½ recipe Basic Pie Dough (page 21)
- 9-inch pie pan

FILLING

- 3 large eggs
- ¾ cup (packed) light brown sugar
- 3 tablespoons all-purpose flour
- 1¼ cups maple syrup
- 4 tablespoons (½ stick) unsalted butter, melted
- ½ teaspoon sea salt
- 2 tablespoons grated orange zest
- 1 teaspoon orange extract
- 1⅓ cups walnuts, chopped
- Whipped cream, for serving (optional)

Preheat the oven to 375°F.

PREPARE THE CRUST

Roll out the dough on a lightly floured surface and fit it into the 9-inch pie pan. Trim the crust overhang to 1 inch and crimp the edges decoratively. Place in the refrigerator.

PREPARE THE FILLING

Beat together the eggs, brown sugar, flour, maple syrup, butter, salt, orange zest and orange extract in a medium-size bowl.

Stir in the chopped nuts.

ASSEMBLE THE PIE

Pour the filling mixture into the chilled crust. Set the pie pan on a rimmed baking sheet and bake 40 to 45 minutes, or until a knife inserted into the center of the pie comes out clean.

Cool completely before serving.

VARIATION: If you'd like a lemony tang instead of an orange one, simply swap out the orange flavoring and zest for equal amounts of lemon flavoring and zest.

WINTER GREENS AND CORNBREAD QUICHE

Cooked winter greens served alongside cornbread is a tried-and-true menu component for many Southern cooks. Why not marry the two together? In this recipe, which makes the most of one of the few greens capable of thriving in cold weather, a quiche filling is crowned with hearty cornbread. Add a glass of Cabernet or dark stout beer and you've got yourself a fireside-worthy meal. For a real "taste of the South," serve with a bit of chow-chow relish. *Makes: 6 to 8 servings*

YOU WILL NEED

9-inch deep-dish pie plate

FILLING

2 tablespoons unsalted butter

¼ cup diced onion

1 bundle of collard greens, chopped (see tip below)

1½ cups chicken or vegetable stock

1 tablespoon malt vinegar (may also substitute apple cider or red or white wine vinegar)

½ teaspoon freshly ground black pepper

8 large eggs, beaten

½ cup heavy cream

½ cup grated cheddar cheese

Dash of hot sauce

½ teaspoon sea salt

CORNBREAD TOPPING

¾ cup cornmeal

½ cup all-purpose flour

2 tablespoons unsalted butter, melted

2 teaspoons baking powder

1 large egg

¾ cup heavy cream or whole milk

½ teaspoon sea salt

1 tablespoon diced jalapeño, (optional)

PREPARE THE FILLING

Melt butter in a large saucepan over medium heat. Add the onion and cook for 2 minutes, or until fragrant. Add the chopped collards and cook for about 4 minutes, until limp, stirring frequently. Add the stock, vinegar, and pepper. Cook, uncovered for 20 to 25 minutes, stirring occasionally, until the liquid has cooked off.

Meanwhile, preheat the oven to 350°F. Butter the 9-inch deep-dish pie plate. Combine the beaten eggs, heavy cream, hot sauce, and salt in a medium-size bowl and whisk to blend.

Pour the mixture into the buttered pie plate. Add the greens, distributing them evenly over the egg mixture. Top with the grated cheese.

Bake for 20 minutes, or until lightly browned, then remove from the oven, leaving the oven on, and set aside.

PREPARE THE CORNBREAD TOPPING

Mix all the topping ingredients in a medium-size bowl until just combined, then spoon evenly over the filling in the pie plate.

BAKE THE QUICHE

Raise the oven temperature to 375°F. Bake the quiche 30 minutes, until the top is lightly golden-brown. Cool 10 or more minutes before serving.

When chopping collards, here's the method I use for making short order of the task: Stack the leaves on top of one another and slice out the rib by cutting on either side. Set the ribs aside, roll the stacked leaves into a tight cylinder, and slice into thin ribbons. Chop the ribbons evenly.

SPICED MEAT PIE

In Britain, and to a large extent, Australia, the term "pie" is synonymous with "meat." This is my homage to such savory victuals. A grown-up version of "sloppy joes," this pie has so much working in its favor. Cloves, cumin, and allspice meet up with brown sugar, ketchup, and red wine under a golden, buttery canopy, creating a complex layer of flavors that's as aromatic as it is tasty. This is the pie that leaves me begging, "More please!" every time it's served. *Makes: 6 servings*

YOU WILL NEED

½ recipe Basic Pie Dough (page 21)

9 x 9-inch baking dish or 9-inch deep-dish pie plate

FILLING

2 tablespoons extra-virgin olive oil

½ cup diced onion

1 medium carrot, diced

2 stalks celery, trimmed and diced

2 cloves garlic, minced

2 pounds ground beef

1 cup vegetable or beef stock

1 can (14 ounces) diced tomatoes

½ cup red wine

1 cup ketchup

½ cup sweet pickle relish

2 tablespoons (packed) dark brown sugar

2 tablespoons Worcestershire sauce

1 teaspoon ground cumin

1 teaspoon dried thyme

1 teaspoon ground allspice

½ teaspoon ground cloves

1 teaspoon sea salt

1 teaspoon freshly ground black pepper

1 teaspoon hot sauce, or to taste

2 tablespoons unsalted butter

2 tablespoons all-purpose flour

Preheat the oven to 375°F. Butter the baking dish or deep-dish pie plate.

PREPARE THE CRUST

Remove the chilled pie dough from the refrigerator and roll out to a 12-inch circle on a lightly floured surface. Transfer the dough to a baking sheet and refrigerate while preparing the filling.

PREPARE THE FILLING

Heat the olive oil in a medium-sized saucepan over medium-high heat. Add the onion, carrot, and celery and sauté 5 minutes. Add the minced garlic and cook another 1 to 2 minutes.

Add the ground beef and cook 4 to 5 minutes until lightly browned.

Add the stock, tomatoes, red wine, ketchup, relish, brown sugar, Worcestershire sauce, cumin, thyme, allspice, cloves, salt, black pepper, and hot sauce. Stir to mix well and cook 20 minutes, stirring occasionally, until fragrant.

In a small saucepan, melt the butter over medium heat and stir in the flour to create a roux. Cook until the mixture turns a light golden brown, stirring constantly.

Stir the roux into the meat mixture and cook over medium-low heat 5 minutes. Remove from the heat.

ASSEMBLE THE PIE

Pour the meat filling into the baking dish or pie plate. Cover with the chilled crust, folding the dough overhang over the edges of the dish and crimp the edges. Cut four to six 2-inch slits in the crust, creating steam vents.

Set the baking dish on a rimmed baking sheet and bake 30 minutes, or until the crust is light golden-brown.

Cool 15 minutes before serving.

VARIATION: For a meatless version, swap out the ground beef with an equal amount of crumbled tempeh. Follow the recipe as directed.

MUSHROOM AND CHEVRE GALETTE

Essentially an open-face pie, galettes are the freeform counterpoint to their pressed and molded kin. In this variation, a filling of mushrooms, herbs, and a bit of chevre is mounded into a flaky rolled crust and baked open-top. While it would serve as a delicious main course, this galette would also be ideal sliced into thin wedges and served as an appetizer. *Makes: 6 to 8 servings*

YOU WILL NEED

½ recipe Basic Pie Dough (page 21)

Large un-rimmed baking sheet

FILLING

4 tablespoons (½ stick) unsalted butter

1 pound mushrooms, sliced (stems and caps)

3 cloves garlic, minced

½ cup red wine

½ cup chicken or vegetable stock

1 tablespoon herbes de Provence (see the tip)

1 teaspoon sea salt

½ teaspoon freshly ground black pepper

½ cup crumbled chevre

1 large egg yolk, beaten

Preheat the oven to 350°F.

PREPARE THE CRUST

Remove the chilled pie dough from the refrigerator and roll out to a 12-inch circle on a lightly floured surface. Transfer the dough to a large un-rimmed baking sheet and refrigerate while you prepare the filling.

PREPARE THE FILLING

Melt the butter in a medium-size saucepan and add mushrooms and garlic. Sauté over medium-low heat for 8 minutes.

Stir in the wine, stock, herbes de Provence, salt, and pepper, then cook 15 minutes, until all the liquid has fully evaporated.

Remove from the heat.

ASSEMBLE THE GALETTE

Spoon the mushroom mixture evenly over the center of chilled pastry circle, leaving a 2-inch border all around. Sprinkle the crumbled chevre evenly over the mushrooms, then fold up the pastry border, overlapping the edges and and pressing the folds together every few inches.

Brush the folded edges of the crust with beaten egg yolk and bake 30 minutes, until the crust is golden.

Cool 30 minutes before serving.

VARIATION: An equal amount of feta cheese can be substituted for the chevre.

TIP — Herbes de Provence is a traditional herbal blend from the southeastern area of France, adjacent to Italy. If you are unable to locate a prepared blend, making your own is easy. Combine and store in a lidded container:

2 tablespoons dried marjoram	1 teaspoon dried basil
2 tablespoons dried thyme	1 teaspoon dried rosemary
2 tablespoons dried savory	1 teaspoon fennel seeds
2 teaspoons dried tarragon	½ teaspoon dried sage

CURRIED WINTER VEGETABLE PIE

When I think of savory winter offerings, I typically think of root vegetables. Potatoes, celeriac, and parsnip, coupled with a bit of curry and garam masala, warm the belly and rouse the taste buds. Just as tasty eaten cold as it is served straight from the oven, this pie works for lunch, brunch, snack, or dinner. Pair it with a shaved fennel and orange salad and watch the snowflakes pile up with a contented sigh. *Makes: 6 to 8 servings*

YOU WILL NEED

- ½ recipe Basic Pie Dough (page 21)
- 9-inch pie pan

FILLING

- 1 pound yellow potatoes (such as Yukon gold), peeled and cubed
- 1 pound celeriac, peeled and cubed (see the tip)
- 1 pound parsnips, peeled and cubed
- 4 large eggs, separated
- 1 cup heavy cream
- 4 tablespoons (½ stick) unsalted butter, melted
- 2 teaspoons sea salt
- 1 teaspoon curry powder
- 1 teaspoon garam masala (see the tip)

EGG WASH

- 1 large egg yolk
- 1 teaspoon water

Preheat the oven to 375°F.

PREPARE THE CRUST

Roll out the dough and fit into the 9-inch pie pan. Trim the crust overhang to 1 inch and crimp the edges decoratively. Place in the refrigerator.

PREPARE THE FILLING

Bring 2 quarts water to a boil in a large saucepan. Add the potatoes and celeriac, and cook for 10 minutes. Add the parsnips and cook for an additional 15 minutes.

Drain the vegetables and place in a large bowl.

In a small bowl, beat the egg yolks. In a separate bowl, whisk egg whites until frothy (beating the whites and yolks separately imparts a bit of lightness into the final pie).

Using a potato masher or large spoon, mash the cooked vegetables with the cream, butter, egg yolks and whites, salt, curry powder, and garam masala.

ASSEMBLE THE PIE

Pour the filling mixture into the chilled crust.

Whisk the egg yolk and water in a small bowl, then use a pastry brush to brush the wash over the edges of the crust.

Set the pie pan on a rimmed baking sheet and bake 45 minutes, until the center of the pie is firm.

Cool before slicing.

A type of celery, celeriac is a root vegetable. Bulbous and gnarly in appearance, celeriac can be found with other root vegetables, such as beets, turnips, and rutabagas, at many grocery stores. Possessing a flavor identical to celery, celeriac must have its outer surface removed prior to use (preferably by slicing the fibrous exterior off with a knife, as peeling the vegetable is a rather challenging task).

An aromatic multi-use spice blend, garam masala is native to northern Indian cuisine. Although the specific composition varies from region to region within India, most garam masalas typically include some blend of peppercorns, cinnamon, cumin, cardamom, nutmeg, star anise, coriander seeds, cloves, mace, and malabar leaves. Look for garam masala at foreign and natural foods stores, or see the Resources section on page 173. If you're unable to find any, simply substitute an equal amount of curry powder.

Tim Mazurek www.lottieanddoof.com

Tim Mazurek is an artist, cook, stylist, and food blogger living on the west side of Chicago with his partner Bryan. Tim's blog, named after his beloved grandmother, Lottie (the "Doof" part is "food" spelled backwards), is gorgeous, inspirational, informative, and just plain fun. He uses Lottie and Doof as a forum for sharing recipes, presenting tantalizing photographs, and opining on "the domestic space as a potentially radical or dangerous space." Here he shares his recipe for Brown Sugar Buttermilk Pie.

BROWN SUGAR BUTTERMILK PIE

Makes: One 9-inch pie

YOU WILL NEED

- ½ recipe Basic Pie Dough (page 21)
  9-inch pie pan

FILLING

- 3 large eggs
- ⅓ cup granulated sugar
- ½ cup (packed) light brown sugar (make sure it is soft!)
- 2 tablespoons all-purpose flour
- 6 tablespoons (¾ stick) unsalted butter, melted and cooled
- 1 cup buttermilk
- 1 teaspoon pure vanilla extract
- ½ teaspoon freshly grated nutmeg
  Pinch of salt

Preheat the oven to 375°F.

PREPARE THE CRUST

Roll out the dough on a lightly floured surface and fit it into the 9–inch pie pan. Trim the crust overhang to 1 inch and crimp the edges decoratively. Refrigerate while you prepare the filling.

PREPARE THE FILLING

In a large bowl, whisk the 3 eggs with both sugars and the flour, making sure there are no lumps. Add the melted butter, buttermilk, vanilla, nutmeg, and salt. Whisk to combine.

ASSEMBLE THE PIE

Pour the filling into the prepared crust and place in the preheated oven.

Turn the oven down to 325°F and bake for 45 to 60 minutes, or until the edges are set and the center is still a little wobbly.

Remove the pie from the oven and let it cool for at least 30 minutes before serving warm or at room temperature.

Leftover pie can be stored in the fridge. It won't be as pretty the next day, but it will be delicious in a whole new way.

Aran Goyoaga www.cannelle-vanille.blogspot.com

Aran Goyoaga is the voice behind the award-winning, highly lauded blog Cannelle et Vanille. A Basque ex-pat living in the U.S. since 1998, Aran uses the site as a stunning showcase of her "recipes, travels, and life stories." In addition to being a gluten-free pastry chef, she is also mother to two little ones and a freelance food writer, stylist, and photographer, as well as cookbook author. Aran's work has garnered a great deal of praise and is considered amongst the finest in the food blog world. Here she shares her recipe for Pear and Hazelnut Frangipane Tart, perfect for wintertime nibbling.

GLUTEN-FREE PEAR AND HAZELNUT FRANGIPANE TART

Makes: One 9-inch tart

YOU WILL NEED

9-inch tart pan
Gluten-free pie dough:
1 cup superfine brown rice flour (see the tip)
2 tablespoons potato starch
2 tablespoons tapioca starch
¼ teaspoon salt
½ cup unsalted butter, cold and diced
3 to 5 tablespoons ice cold water

PEAR AND HAZELNUT
FRANGIPANE FILLING

½ cup unsalted butter, room temperature
½ cup cane sugar
1 large egg
1 cup hazelnut flour (see the tip)
1 tablespoon tapioca starch
Pinch of salt
1 tablespoon dark rum, optional

7 Forelle pears, halved and core removed
Powdered sugar, for sprinkling

PREPARE THE PIE DOUGH

Place the first four ingredients in a food processor and pulse a couple of times to combine.

Add the cold, diced butter and pulse 10 times, until the butter is cut into the flours.

TIP Whole Foods and many supermarkets carry these flours. Otherwise they can be ordered online through Bob's Red Mill or Authentic Foods.

Add the ice water while pulsing. You might not need all of it, so reserve a couple of tablespoons until mixed. The dough should stick together when pressed but not be too wet.

Form the dough into a disk, wrap it in plastic wrap, and flatten it a bit with your hand. Refrigerate the dough for about 1 hour.

Preheat the oven to 375°F.

Roll out the dough to about ¼- to ⅛-inch thickness and fill the 9-inch tart pan with it. If the dough cracks, don't worry, just pinch it back together. (This might happen if the dough is too cold.)

Return the tart pan to the refrigerator for another 20 minutes or so.

Meanwhile, roll the leftover dough scraps and cut shapes with star cookie cutters. Place on a baking sheet lined with parchment and bake for about 8 minutes. Set the star cookies aside to use later, and reduce the oven temperature to 350°F.

PREPARE THE FILLING

Cream the butter and sugar together until light.
Add the egg and mix.

Add the rest of the ingredients and mix until combined.

ASSEMBLE THE TART

Spread the frangipane inside the tart crust.

Cut the pears into thin slices lengthwise and place them on top of the frangipane.

Bake in the middle of the 350°F oven for about 30 to 40 minutes, until the filling is brown and the bottom of the tart is cooked.

SPRING

Crocuses and daffodils and green buds galore! Spring is quite literally a breath of very fresh, very welcome air after winter's gray bluster. While farmers' markets and gardens may not yet be busting at the seams with a full harvest, there are a number of crops available that will imbue pies with seasonal flavor and pizzazz. By the end of June, when summer is knocking on the door and spring is bidding farewell, the season's offerings will have increased exponentially, inviting all sorts of scrumptious pie and tart making opportunities!

APRICOTS * ASPARAGUS * CARROTS * CELERY
DILL * EGGS * FRESH CHEESE * LEEKS
NEW POTATOES * PEAS * RHUBARB
SPINACH * STRAWBERRIES
THYME * WATERCRESS

STRAWBERRY CRUMBLE PIE WITH LEMON VERBENA WHIPPED CREAM

Lemon verbena is, hands down, one of my most favorite herbs. It imbues everything it accompanies with the most exquisite lemon-y flavor. Here I've used it to infuse heavy cream, which is then beaten into billowy clouds of herbaceous whipped goodness. A healthy dollop atop this crumble-topped strawberry pie might just make lemon verbena your favorite herb, too!

Makes: One 9-inch pie

YOU WILL NEED

- ½ recipe Basic Pie Dough (page 21)
- 9-inch pie pan

WHIPPED TOPPING

- 1 cup heavy cream
- 2 tablespoons fresh lemon verbena, finely chopped
- 3 tablespoons powdered sugar (added after steeping)

FILLING

- 1½ pounds strawberries, stemmed and halved
- ⅓ cup cornstarch
- ⅓ cup granulated sugar

CRUMBLE TOPPING

- ¾ cup all-purpose flour
- ½ teaspoon sea salt
- ½ cup (packed) light brown sugar
- 6 tablespoons (¾ stick) unsalted butter, cubed

START THE WHIPPED TOPPING

Combine the heavy cream and lemon verbena in a lidded container, such as a mason jar. Shake the contents vigorously.

Place the mixture in the refrigerator and steep for at least 4 hours.

Preheat oven to 400°F.

PREPARE THE CRUST

Roll out the dough on a lightly floured surface and fit it into the 9-inch pie pan. Trim the crust overhang to 1 inch and crimp the edges decoratively. Prick the bottom of the crust 6 or 7 times with a fork, then place the crust in the refrigerator for 15 minutes.

Line the crust with parchment paper and fill it with dried beans or pie weights. Bake 10 to 12 minutes, and then remove from the oven, leaving the oven on.

Remove the dried beans or pie weights and parchment paper from the crust, and cool it completely before filling.

PREPARE THE FILLING

Combine the strawberries, cornstarch and sugar in a medium-size bowl. Set aside.

PREPARE THE CRUMBLE TOPPING

Combine the flour, salt, brown sugar, and butter in a medium-size bowl. Crumble together with either your hands or a pastry blender, leaving pea-sized chunks of butter in the mixture. Set aside.

ASSEMBLE THE PIE

Pour the strawberry mixture into the crust. Sprinkle the crumble topping evenly over the surface, packing down as needed to accommodate the entire amount.

Set the pie pan on a rimmed baking sheet and bake for 40 to 45 minutes, until the topping is golden brown. Cool the pie at least 1 hour before serving.

FINISH THE WHIPPED TOPPING

Strain the contents of the jar containing the cream and lemon verbena through a fine-mesh sieve. Discard the lemon verbena.

Using either a mixer or whisk, beat the infused cream and powdered sugar until billowy peaks form. Serve alongside the pie.

VARIATION: If lemon verbena is unavailable, substitute an equal amount of fresh lemongrass or lemon balm for a similar lemon taste.

FROZEN STRAWBERRY PIE

This is my attempt at recreating a pie from my youth. When I was around 10 years old, my good friend Erica and her older sister made a yogurt and fresh strawberry frozen pie that was the very definition of spring. My version includes the addition of heavy cream and cradles the entire ethereal concoction in a homemade graham-cracker crust. While opting for a pre-made version might be tempting, resist! This crust is the absolute perfect ratio of sweet-crunchy harmony. Although Erica and I long ago fell out of touch, I like to think that, should she happen upon this recipe, she'd feel I did her beloved pie justice. *Makes: One 9-inch pie*

YOU WILL NEED

Graham Cracker Crust (page 23)

9-inch pie pan

FILLING

2 cups whole-milk vanilla yogurt

3 tablespoons honey

2 cups strawberries, hulled and sliced

1 cup heavy cream

1 teaspoon vanilla extract

OPTIONAL GARNISH

½ cup strawberries, hulled and thinly sliced

PREPARE THE FILLING

Combine the yogurt and honey in a large bowl. Stir in the 2 cups strawberries.

In a medium-size bowl, using a mixer or a whisk, beat the cream and vanilla until billowy peaks form.

Fold the whipped cream into the strawberry mixture.

ASSEMBLE THE PIE

Pour the filling mixture into the cooled crust. If desired, arrange sliced strawberries in a circle around the outer edge of the pie.

Freeze at least 4 hours before serving.

VARIATION: This pie can also be made during the summer months, replacing the strawberries with an equal quantity of blackberries or raspberries.

Frozen Strawberry Pie

HONEY PIE

Given a good supply of available nectar, honeybees will have honey ready to harvest in late spring. This custard-based pie showcases honey's ambrosial qualities with every bite. Incredibly easy to make, this pie would make a wonderful gift for your own "sweetie." If you want to really gild the lily, serve a slice with a small glass of honey mead. *Makes: One 9-inch pie*

YOU WILL NEED

- ½ recipe Basic Pie Dough (page 21)
- 9-inch pie pan

FILLING

- 1 cup whole milk
- 4 large eggs, at room temperature
- ½ cup honey
- 2 teaspoons vanilla extract
- Pinch of sea salt
- Freshly grated nutmeg

Preheat the oven to 400°F.

PREPARE THE CRUST

Roll out the dough on a lightly floured surface and fit it into the 9-inch pie pan. Trim the crust overhang to 1 inch and crimp the edges decoratively. Prick the bottom of the crust 6 to 7 times with a fork, then place the crust in the refrigerator for 15 minutes.

Line the crust with parchment paper and fill it with dried beans or pie weights. Bake 10 to 12 minutes, then remove from the oven, leaving the oven on at 400°F.

Remove the dried beans or pie weights and parchment paper from the crust, and cool it completely before filling.

PREPARE THE FILLING

Warm the milk in a small saucepan over medium heat. Watch carefully and remove the pan from the heat just before bubbles begin forming on the surface of the milk. Set aside.

Whisk the eggs, honey, vanilla, and salt in a medium-size bowl. Add the warmed milk to the egg mixture slowly, whisking in a bit at a time before adding more.

Once all of the milk is added to the egg mixture, whisk thoroughly to make sure all the ingredients are fully incorporated.

ASSEMBLE THE PIE

Pour the filling mixture into the prepared crust, then grate fresh nutmeg liberally over the surface.

Place the pie pan on a rimmed baking sheet and bake for 30 minutes.

Cool at least 1 hour before serving.

VARIATION: For an orange-flavored honey pie, replace the vanilla extract with an equal amount of orange extract.

LATTICE-TOP RHUBARB, LEMON, AND VANILLA PIE

Though technically a vegetable, rhubarb has earned its rightful place in the pantheon of sweet pies. Thus, as one of the first "fruits" of spring, its sight makes many bakers rush to their rolling pins in delight. Here I've partnered the puckery fruit with a healthy dose of lemon zest and juice and just a kiss of nutmeg. Although you might be tempted to slice into it as soon as its ruby-red gloriousness comes out of the oven, do allow it adequate time to cool. Once the bottom of the pie pan is no longer warm to the touch, break out the pie server and slice away! *Makes: One 9-inch pie*

YOU WILL NEED

- 1 recipe Basic Pie Dough (page 21)
- 9-inch pie pan

FILLING

- 1½ pounds rhubarb, trimmed and chopped into ½-inch pieces
- 1⅓ cups granulated sugar
- ½ cup arrowroot powder or cornstarch
- Grated zest and juice of 1 lemon
- 2 teaspoons vanilla extract
- ½ teaspoon ground nutmeg

EGG WASH:

- 1 large egg yolk
- 1 tablespoon cold water

- 2 tablespoons turbinado sugar or other coarse sugar, for sprinkling

 TIP Work quickly when cutting and assembling the lattice top. Sugar is hygroscopic, meaning it pulls moisture out of other materials and into itself. Therefore, the less time that the rhubarb and the sugar interact before going into the hot oven to bake, the better.

PREPARE THE CRUST

Remove one dough disk from the refrigerator. Roll out the dough on a lightly floured surface and fit it into the 9-inch pie pan. Trim the crust overhang to 1 inch, then place the crust in the refrigerator while you prepare the filling.

PREPARE THE FILLING

Place the chopped rhubarb, sugar, arrowroot or cornstarch, lemon zest and juice, vanilla extract, and nutmeg in a medium-size bowl. Stir together with a large spoon until well combined.

Pour the rhubarb filling into the chilled crust.

ASSEMBLE THE PIE

Preheat the oven to 425°F.

Roll the remaining dough disk into a 12-inch circle. Using a pastry wheel, cut twelve 1-inch-wide strips of dough. (I like to use the fluted edge of the pastry wheel, but you can use the smooth wheel, if you prefer.)

Arrange the lattice strips over the pie filling in alternating rows, weaving six strips horizontally and six vertically (see page 31 for detailed latticing instructions).

Trim the lattice strips to a 1-inch overhang and tuck the top and bottom overhangs under the bottom crust. Crimp the edges decoratively as desired.

Whisk the egg yolk and water together in a small bowl, then use a pastry brush to brush the wash over the lattice and the edges of the crust. Sprinkle the turbinado or other coarse sugar over the pie.

Transfer the pie pan to a rimmed baking sheet lined with parchment paper or aluminum foil to catch overflow juices. Bake for 1 hour, until the crust is golden and juices are bubbling in the center of the pie.

Cool at least 4 hours before serving.

VARIATION: Trade an equal amount of orange juice and zest for the lemon juice and zest, and replace the nutmeg with 1 teaspoon of ground cinnamon.

CARROT PIE

One of my favorite things about going out for Indian food is the array of desserts available. My pie tribute to carrot halwa—a mixture of carrots, dried fruits, and spices—this recipe pairs the sweet vegetable with classic Indian flavors of cardamom, ginger, cinnamon, and black pepper. Think "pumpkin pie goes to Mumbai" to get a sense of its flavor profile. *Makes: One 9-inch pie*

YOU WILL NEED

½ recipe Basic Pie Dough (page 21)

9-inch pie pan

FILLING

1 pound carrots, scrubbed and ends removed

½ cup (packed) light brown sugar

1 cup whole milk

1 teaspoon ground cardamom

½ teaspoon ground ginger

½ teaspoon ground cinnamon

½ teaspoon freshly ground black pepper

½ teaspoon sea salt

3 large eggs, separated

Preheat the oven to 400°F.

PREPARE THE CRUST

Roll out the dough on a lightly floured surface and fit it into the 9-inch pie pan. Trim the crust overhang to 1 inch and crimp the edges decoratively. Prick the bottom of the crust 6 or 7 times with a fork, then place the crust in the refrigerator for 15 minutes.

Line the crust with parchment paper and fill it with dried beans or pie weights. Bake 10 to 12 minutes, then remove the crust from the oven, leaving the oven on and reducing the temperature to 350°F.

Remove the dried beans or pie weights and parchment paper from the crust, and cool it completely before filling.

PREPARE THE FILLING

Cut the prepped carrots into ¼-inch rounds. Steam them in a saucepan in 1 inch of water for 5 minutes, until slightly softened. Drain off the water in a colander, then puree the carrots in a blender or food processor until completely smooth.

Add the sugar, milk, spices, and salt to the carrots in the processor and puree until well combined. Pour the mixture into a medium-size bowl.

Whisk the egg yolks in a small bowl until blended. Using either a whisk or an electric mixer, beat the egg whites in a separate bowl until foamy.

Whisk the beaten egg yolks into the carrot puree until well blended, then whisk in the beaten whites. This isn't a soufflé, so don't worry about being gentle with the whites when you incorporate them into the purée.

ASSEMBLE THE PIE

Pour the carrot purée into the prepared crust. Set the pie pan on a rimmed baking sheet and bake in the 375°F oven for 40 to 45 minutes, until the filling is set.

Cool for at least 30 minutes before serving.

VARIATION: For a more traditionally spiced pie, omit the cardamom and black pepper, increase the cinnamon to 1 teaspoon, and add ½ teaspoon each ground nutmeg and ground cloves.

FIADONE

Also known as "ricotta pie," fiadone is a traditional Italian ricotta-based pie. It is most commonly served around Easter in southern Italy, with regional variations in flavor additions. Some include candied citrus, while others use chocolate, nuts, or, as in this recipe, raisins and lemons. I opted to jazz up the traditional version a bit by including anise seeds, a spice often employed in Italian dessert making. The result is a creamy, custardy pie that epitomizes all of the freshness and flavor of springtime. Though delicious warm, I think this pie truly shines once chilled. *Makes: One 9-inch pie*

YOU WILL NEED

½ recipe Basic Pie Dough (page 21)

9-inch pie pan

FILLING

3 large eggs

⅔ cup granulated sugar

1 pound ricotta cheese

¼ cup heavy cream

Grated zest and juice of 1 lemon

1 teaspoon anise seeds

2 teaspoons vanilla extract

¼ cup golden raisins

Preheat the oven to 400°F.

PREPARE THE CRUST

Roll out the dough on a lightly floured surface and fit it into the 9-inch pie pan. Trim the crust overhang to 1 inch and crimp edges decoratively. Prick the bottom of the crust 6 or 7 times with a fork, then place the crust in the refrigerator for 15 minutes.

Line the crust with parchment paper and fill it with dried beans or pie weights. Bake 10 to 12 minutes, then remove from the oven, leaving the oven on and reducing the temperature to 350°F.

Remove the dried beans or pie weights and parchment paper from the crust, and cool it completely before filling.

PREPARE THE FILLING

Using either an electric mixer or a whisk, beat the eggs in a medium-size bowl until light and fluffy.

Add the sugar and continue beating until the sugar is fully blended into the eggs, then add the ricotta cheese and heavy cream. Beat for 2 minutes until completely blended.

Add the lemon zest, lemon juice, anise seeds, and vanilla extract and beat 1 to 2 minutes longer. Stir in the raisins, using a large spoon.

ASSEMBLE THE PIE

Pour the filling mixture into the prepared crust. Set the pie pan on a rimmed baking sheet and bake in the 350°F oven for 45 minutes, or until the filling is firm (when a knife inserted in the center comes out clean).

Cool at least 1 hour before serving. This pie is particularly good after chilling.

VARIATION: Replace the raisins with an equal amount of candied lemon peel.

APRICOT ALMOND GALETTE

You want to be sure to select ripe apricots for this galette. Otherwise, the inherent "puckeriness" of apricots will make it much too tart. When selecting fruits, use those that offer a little "give" when gently pressed. Ripe apricots also smell sweet. If there's no telltale fragrance, keep searching.

Makes: 8 to 10 servings

YOU WILL NEED

½ recipe Basic Pie Dough (page 21)

Un-rimmed baking sheet

FILLING

2 pounds apricots

½ cup granulated sugar

¼ cup arrowroot powder or cornstarch

2 teaspoons ground coriander

⅓ teaspoon sea salt

2 tablespoons unsalted butter, diced, for dotting the filling

EGG WASH

1 large egg yolk

1 tablespoon cold water

ALMOND TOPPING

½ cup sliced almonds

2 tablespoons turbinado sugar or other coarse sugar

Preheat the oven to 425°F.

PREPARE THE CRUST

Remove the chilled pie dough from the refrigerator and roll it out into a 12-inch circle on a lightly floured surface. Transfer the crust to an un-rimmed baking sheet and return it to the refrigerator to chill while preparing the filling.

PREPARE THE FILLING

Cut the apricots in half and remove the pits. Next, cut each half into quarters, and then slice the quarters into eighths.

Combine the sugar, arrowroot or cornstarch, coriander, and salt in a medium-size bowl. Add the apricot slices, and using either clean hands or a large spoon, toss all the ingredients together.

ASSEMBLE THE GALETTE

Mound the apricot mixture in the middle of the chilled pastry circle, leaving a small amount of the juices from the mixture in the bowl (you'll be tossing the juices with the sliced almonds later). Gently spread the mixture out toward the edge of the pastry, leaving a 2-inch border all around.

Dot the surface of the galette with the diced butter. Fold the pastry border up over the filling, overlapping the edges and pressing the folds together every few inches.

Whisk the egg yolk and water in a small bowl, then use a pastry brush to brush the wash over the folded edges of the crust.

Bake at 425°F for 20 minutes, then reduce the oven temperature to 375°F and bake for another 15 minutes.

Remove the galette from the oven, leaving the oven on. Toss the sliced almonds with the reserved apricot mixture juice and spread them evenly over the surface of the galette, then sprinkle the coarse sugar over both the almonds and the pastry crust.

Return the galette to the oven and bake for 15 minutes longer until the fruit juices in the center are bubbling and the almonds are browned.

Cool the galette at least 30 minutes before serving.

STRAWBERRY, RHUBARB, AND GINGER HAND PIES

Springtime is my favorite time of year for picnics. It's neither too hot nor too cool for lying about outdoors. It's also strawberry season, and I can think of few foods that yell "picnic" louder than strawberries. In this recipe, I've partnered the beloved berry with its ideal baking partner, rhubarb, added a healthy dose of crystallized ginger and wrapped the whole concoction up in crescents of dough, creating eminently transportable hand pies. The result is a sweet-sour-spicy trifecta that will leave you wishing spring, and strawberry season, would stick around all year. *Makes: 16 hand pies*

YOU WILL NEED

- 1 recipe Basic Pie Dough (page 21)
- 5-inch circular cookie cutter
- 2 cookie sheets lined with parchment paper or a silicone mat

FILLING

- 2 cups rhubarb, trimmed and cut into 1-inch pieces (between 2 to 4 stalks, depending on thickness)
- 2 cups strawberries, stemmed and quartered
- ½ cup granulated sugar
- ¼ cup cornstarch
- 2 tablespoons lemon juice
- ¼ cup minced crystallized ginger

EGG WASH

- 1 large egg yolk
- 1 tablespoon whole milk
- ⅓ cup demerara sugar or other coarse sugar, for sprinkling

PREPARE THE HAND PIECRUSTS

Remove one disk of the chilled pie dough from the refrigerator and roll it out into a 12- to 14-inch circle on a lightly floured surface.

Cut out eight 5-inch rounds using a circular cookie cutter. Re-roll scraps as necessary. Transfer the dough rounds to one of the lined cookie sheets. Repeat with the second chilled dough disk, transferring the finished 8 dough rounds to the second lined cookie sheet.

Refrigerate the sheets of dough rounds while you prepare the filling.

PREPARE THE FILLING

Place all the ingredients for the filling in a large bowl. Toss with either your hands or a large spoon until well combined. Cover the bowl with a kitchen cloth and set aside for 30 minutes.

Pour the mixture into a colander and drain off any liquid that has been produced. Don't press down on the fruits; simply allow anything formed while the mixture sat to drain away.

ASSEMBLE THE HAND PIES

Preheat the oven to 350°F.

Remove the cookie sheets containing the chilled dough rounds from the refrigerator.

Mound 2 to 3 tablespoons of the strawberry-rhubarb mixture on the right side of each dough round, leaving about a ¼-inch border around the edge.

Fold the left half of each dough round over to cover the fruit mixture completely, then press the edges with the tines of a fork to seal, forming a half-moon.

Return the pies to the refrigerator and chill for 20 minutes.

Whisk the egg yolk and milk in a small bowl, then use a pastry brush to brush the wash lightly over the top of each hand pie.

Sprinkle the pies with about 2 teaspoons each of the demerara sugar and bake for 25 to 30 minutes, until the crusts are golden brown.

Cool for at least 30 minutes before serving.

COCONUT CREAM PIE WITH VANILLA BEAN WHIPPED TOPPING

While not necessarily "seasonal," coconut cream pie is often linked to spring months and festivities, as are a number of other coconut-based desserts. In this recipe, a rich custard base is topped by vanilla bean-scented whipped cream. If you can find a fresh coconut–and want to make the effort–large flakes peeled from fresh coconut meat and then toasted make for a dramatic, and delicious, finishing touch. *Makes: One 9-inch pie*

YOU WILL NEED:

- ½ recipe Basic Pie Dough (page 21)
-    9-inch pie pan

WHIPPED TOPPING

- 1 vanilla bean
- 1½ cups heavy cream
- 3 tablespoons powdered sugar (added after steeping)

FILLING

- ¾ cup granulated sugar
- 3 tablespoons cornstarch
- ½ teaspoon sea salt
- 2 cups whole milk
- 3 large egg yolks, beaten
- 1 cup sweetened flaked coconut
- 1 teaspoon vanilla extract
- 1 teaspoon coconut extract
- 3 tablespoons unsalted butter
- ¼ cup sweetened flaked coconut, lightly toasted (to serve)

START THE WHIPPED TOPPING

Slice the vanilla bean open, and using the tip of a paring knife, scrape out the seeds inside. Combine the seeds with the heavy cream in a lidded container, such as a mason jar. Shake the contents vigorously.

Place the mixture in the refrigerator and steep for at least 4 hours.

PREPARE THE CRUST

Preheat the oven to 400°F.

Roll out the dough on a lightly floured surface and fit it into the 9-inch pie pan. Trim the crust overhang to 1 inch and crimp the edges decoratively. Prick the bottom of the crust 6 or 7 times with a fork, then place the crust in the refrigerator for 15 minutes.

Line the crust with parchment paper and fill it with dried beans or pie weights. Bake for 12 to 15 minutes, then remove from the oven, leaving the oven on.

Remove the dried beans or pie weights and parchment paper from the crust, then return it to the oven and bake an additional 5 to 7 minutes, until the crust is golden.

Cool completely before filling.

PREPARE THE FILLING

Combine the sugar, cornstarch, and salt in a medium-size saucepan. Add the milk and bring to a boil. Cook 2 minutes, stirring constantly. Turn the heat to low.

Remove ½ cup of the cooked mixture and pour it slowly over the beaten egg yolks in a small bowl, whisking constantly until thoroughly combined.

 It's essential that you take your time when adding the cooked mixture to the eggs, otherwise they'll curdle. Pour it in a gentle, steady stream, whisking vigorously the entire time.

Return the egg yolk mixture to the saucepan on the stove. Cook over medium-low heat for 2 to 3 minutes, whisking constantly.

Remove the mixture from the heat and whisk in the extracts and butter. Beat until the butter is fully melted and the mixture is smooth. Stir in the coconut.

Transfer the coconut custard to a medium-size glass or ceramic bowl. Cover and allow to come to room temperature.

Once cooled, pour it into the cooled crust, using a spatula as necessary to distribute the custard evenly.

FINISH THE WHIPPED TOPPING

Pour the infused cream into a medium-size bowl. Add the powdered sugar, and using either a mixer or whisk, beat the infused cream and powdered sugar until billowy peaks form.

ASSEMBLE THE PIE

Pile the whipped topping over the pie, mounding in the center and covering the filling completely. Sprinkle the toasted flaked coconut evenly across the top.

Place the pie in the refrigerator and keep chilled until ready to serve.

Coconut Cream Pie with Vanilla Bean Whipped Topping

SPINACH, POTATO, AND CHEESE PIE

Essentially a strata, with phyllo dough in place of the more traditional bread slices, this pie is the ideal "anytime" pie. From breakfast to brunch, lunch to dinner, this recipe is substantive enough to satisfy at any meal. The inspiration came from my husband's aunt and her recipe for spanikopita. While this recipe contains a number of ingredients used in that dish, it contains individual layers instead of a mixture, allowing each element to truly shine. *Makes: 12 servings*

YOU WILL NEED

13 x 9-inch baking pan

FILLING

5 tablespoons olive oil

1 pound thin-skinned, medium-starch potatoes, such as Yukon Gold, scrubbed and cut into ⅓-inch slices

4 slices thick-cut bacon, cooked and crumbled

1 cup chopped spring onions or scallions

2 pounds fresh baby spinach, washed and drained

3 large eggs

1 pound ricotta cheese

1 teaspoon sea salt

Freshly ground black pepper

PHYLLO

1 pound phyllo pastry

8 tablespoons (1 stick) unsalted butter, melted

ASSEMBLY

1 cup grated Manchego cheese

3 hard-boiled eggs, sliced

1 cup crumbled feta cheese

1 tablespoon chopped fresh dill

Preheat the oven to 350°F. Butter the baking pan and set aside.

PREPARE THE FILLING

Heat 2 tablespoons of the olive oil in a medium-size skillet over medium-low heat. Add the potato slices and cook for 15 minutes, turning the slices over every couple of minutes, until they're browned evenly on both sides. Remove the pan from heat, take the potato slices out of the pan and set aside.

In a separate skillet, cook the bacon until crisp. Drain off the excess fat once cooked by placing the bacon slices on a paper towel until slightly cool. Crumble the bacon into small pieces. Transfer the crumbles to a small bowl and set aside.

Heat the remaining 3 tablespoons olive oil in a medium-size saucepan. Add the spring onions and cook for 5 minutes over medium-low heat.

Add the spinach and stir until well coated with oil, then cook, uncovered, until it is fully wilted and the liquid has cooked off, about 5 to 7 minutes.

Remove the saucepan from the heat. Transfer the spinach mixture to a medium-size bowl and set aside.

Whisk the eggs in a medium-size bowl. Stir in the ricotta cheese, along with the salt and a few grinds of black pepper. Set aside.

ASSEMBLE THE PIE

One at a time, brush half the phyllo sheets with butter, and layer them in the bottom of the baking dish. Arrange the potato slices atop the phyllo dough, evenly spaced, and sprinkle evenly with the grated Manchego cheese. Spoon half of the spinach mixture evenly over the cheese.

Arrange the egg slices evenly over the spinach and sprinkle with the crumbled bacon. Spoon the rest of the spinach evenly over the bacon and sprinkle with the crumbled feta. Pour the ricotta mixture evenly over the feta and smooth out with a spatula. Sprinkle the chopped dill evenly over the ricotta.

Brush each of the remaining sheets of phyllo with butter and layer over the ricotta. Fold in the overlapping phyllo edges and brush the entire top liberally with butter.

Bake for 50 minutes, until the top is golden brown.

Cool at least one hour before serving.

Variation: For a vegetarian dish, replace the bacon with an equal amount of smoky tempeh "bacon" strips.

VARIATION: For a vegetarian dish, replace the bacon with an equal amount of smoky tempeh "bacon" strips.

Spinach, Potato, and Cheese Pie

CHICKEN POT PIE

This top-crust chicken pot pie is rife with springtime pickings, including peas, celery, carrots, onions, and fresh thyme. My good friend Jodi Rhoden, proprietress of Short Street Cakes here in Asheville, is the person responsible for giving me the genius idea of adding celery seeds to the crust itself. After the chilled pie dough is rolled out, the seeds are sprinkled over it and then embedded with a few pats from the rolling pin. I love this pie on still-chilly spring evenings, when a cardigan and a strong, stout beer are completely in order. *Makes: 6 servings*

YOU WILL NEED

½ recipe Basic Pie Dough (page 21)

1 teaspoon celery seed

9 x 9 inch baking dish or 9-inch deep-dish pie plate

Large un-rimmed baking sheet

FILLING

8 tablespoons (1 stick) unsalted butter

1 medium onion, diced

3 carrots, peeled and cut into ¼-inch rounds

1½ cups sliced mushrooms

1 stalk celery, trimmed and diced

2 cloves garlic, minced (see tip below)

1 cup fresh peas

½ cup all-purpose flour

2 cups chicken stock

½ cup rosé or white wine

½ cup half-and-half

2 teaspoons chopped fresh thyme (or 1 teaspoon dried)

1 pound meat from a roasted chicken, shredded into bite-size pieces

EGG WASH

1 large egg yolk

1 tablespoon cold water

Butter the 9 x 9-inch baking dish or deep-dish pie plate. Set aside.

PREPARE THE CRUST

Remove the chilled pie dough from the refrigerator and roll it out into a 12-inch circle on a lightly floured surface. Sprinkle the celery seeds across the surface of the dough and roll over it lightly several times with the rolling pin until the seeds are imbedded in the dough.

Transfer the dough circle to a large unrimmed baking sheet and refrigerate while preparing the filling.

PREPARE THE FILLING

Melt 2 tablespoons of the butter in a medium-size saucepan over medium-low heat. Add the onion, carrots, mushrooms, celery, and garlic and sauté for 15 minutes, stirring frequently, until softened and lightly browned.

Add the peas and cook for 5 more minutes, then remove from the heat and transfer to a medium-size bowl. Set aside.

Preheat the oven to 375°F.

Melt the remaining 6 tablespoons butter in the same saucepan, then add the flour.

Stir constantly for about 2 minutes, until the mixture turns a sort of blond color.

Little by little, stir in the chicken stock, whisking with each addition to create a creamy sauce.

Whisk in the wine, half-and-half, and thyme, then cook, stirring frequently, 10 minutes longer until thickened. Return the vegetable mixture to the saucepan, along with the shredded chicken, and stir until everything is fully coated with the sauce.

ASSEMBLE THE PIE

Pour the chicken and vegetable mixture into the prepared baking dish or pie plate and cover with the chilled piecrust. Fold the dough overhang over on the edges of the dish and crimp decoratively as desired.

Whisk the egg yolk and water in a small bowl, then use a pastry brush to brush the wash over the edges of the crust. Cut four to six 2-inch slits in the crust, creating steam vents. You'll need to work quickly while doing this, as the warm chicken and vegetable mixture will heat up the dough, potentially causing the fat within it to melt.

Set the baking dish on a rimmed baking sheet and bake for 30 minutes, until the crust is golden brown.

Cool at least 20 minute before serving.

 Mincing the garlic at the beginning of the cooking process, and allowing it to "sit" for at least 10 minutes before use, helps its flavor mellow a bit. This can be particularly helpful to those who are sensitive to the volatile oils in the plant.

ASPARAGUS AND DILL QUICHE

Asparagus is perhaps the quintessential spring vegetable. Available fresh for only a handful of weeks, nothing beats its earthy, fresh taste. Partnered up with fresh dill and feta cheese, this quiche might just become your go-to dish of the season. It's incredibly easy to put together and packs a serious springtime flavor punch. *Makes: One 9-inch pie*

YOU WILL NEED

- ½ recipe Basic Pie Dough (page 21)
- 9-inch pie pan

FILLING

- 1 pound asparagus, trimmed of tough ends and cut into 2-inch segments
- 6 large eggs
- ½ cup heavy cream
- 1 teaspoon sea salt
- 2 teaspoons chopped fresh dill (or 1 teaspoon dried)
- ½ cup crumbled feta cheese

Preheat the oven to 400°F.

PREPARE THE CRUST

Roll out the dough and fit it into the 9-inch pie pan. Trim the crust overhang to 1 inch and crimp the edges decoratively. Prick the bottom of the crust 6 or 7 times with a fork, then place the crust in the refrigerator for 15 minutes.

Line the crust with parchment paper and fill it with dried beans or pie weights. Bake 10 to 12 minutes, then remove from the oven, leaving the oven on and reducing the temperature to 375°F.

Remove the dried beans or pie weights and parchment paper from the crust, and cool it completely before filling.

PREPARE THE FILLING

Bring 2 quarts of water to a boil in a large saucepan

Add the asparagus pieces to the boiling water, and after the water returns to the boil, cook for 5 minutes.

Drain the asparagus, rinse with cold water, and set aside.

In a medium-size bowl, whisk the eggs until blended, then whisk in the cream, together with the salt, to blend well. Set aside.

ASSEMBLE THE QUICHE

Line the sides of the crust by propping asparagus pieces solidly up against them. Use the remaining asparagus to fill in the middle, radiating out from the center.

Sprinkle the dill over the asparagus in the pie shell, then gently pour the egg mixture over the asparagus; the asparagus around the rim should stick out above the surface of the egg mixture.

Sprinkle the feta evenly over the top.

Set the pie pan on a rimmed baking sheet and bake in the 375°F oven for 45 minutes.

Cool for at least 30 minutes before serving.

VARIATION: Crumbled goat cheese may be substituted for the feta.

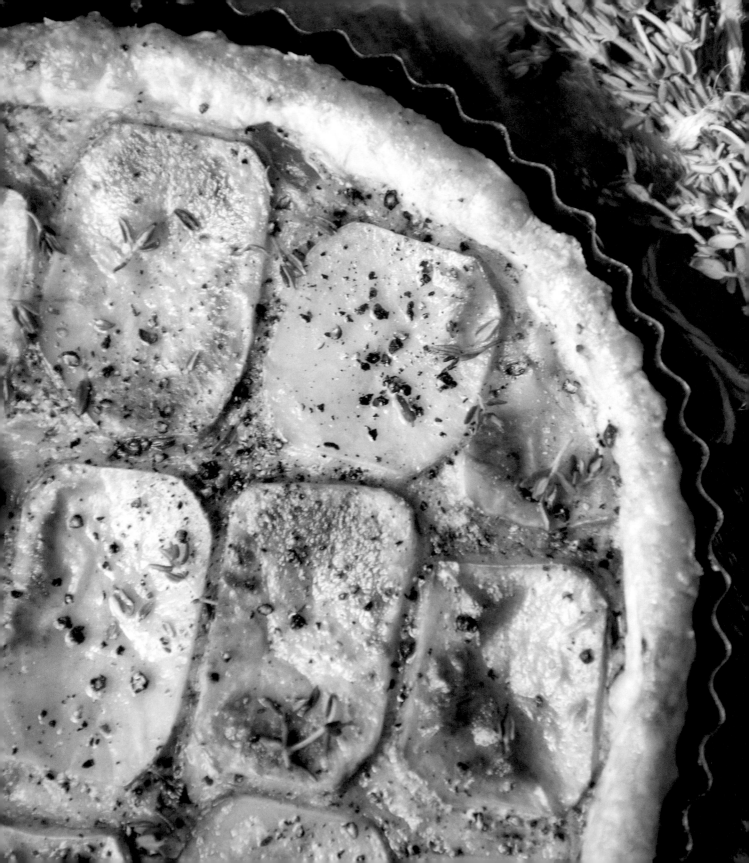

LEEK AND POTATO TART

This tart is just as impressive in its presentation as it is delicious. A grid of potatoes tops a bed of caramelized leeks, fresh thyme, and an egg-and-cream blend. Pair a slice of this with an arugula salad and a crisp Sauvignon Blanc for a heavenly springtime meal. This tart would also make a beautiful offering to bring to a Mother's Day or Easter brunch or luncheon. *Makes: One 8-inch tart*

YOU WILL NEED

½ recipe Basic Pie Dough (page 21)

8-inch tart pan with removable bottom

FILLING

6 medium-size leeks

2 tablespoons unsalted butter

2 tablespoons olive oil, plus extra for the baking sheet

1½ cups chicken or vegetable stock

½ cup white or rosé wine

2 tablespoons (packed) light brown sugar

2 medium-size red-skinned potatoes

2 large eggs

½ cup heavy cream

Pinch of sea salt

1 tablespoon chopped fresh thyme leaves or 1 teaspoon dried

1 teaspoon freshly ground black pepper

EGG WASH

1 large egg yolk

1 tablespoon cold water

Preheat the oven to 400°F.

PREPARE THE CRUST

Roll out the dough on a lightly floured surface and fit it into the 8-inch tart pan. Trim the overhang to 1 inch, then fold it inside the tart pan, pressing it against the pan's fluted sides. Prick the bottom of the crust 6 or 7 times with a fork, then place the crust in the refrigerator for 15 minutes.

Line the crust with parchment paper and fill it with dried beans or pie weights. Bake 10 minutes, then remove from the oven.

Remove the dried beans or pie weights and parchment paper from the crust, and cool it for 15 to 20 minutes before filling.

PREPARE THE FILLING

Cut off the top portion of each leek, right down to where the stalk turns light green. Cut off the root end as well. Slice the remaining stalk into ½-inch rounds.

Put the rounds into a large bowl of water, separating the rings in each round by pushing out the middle with your fingers. Remove the leeks to a colander, then rinse well again under cold running water to remove any lingering dirt. Drain.

Heat the butter and olive oil in a medium-size saucepan over medium-low heat. Add the leeks and cook, stirring frequently for about 15 minutes, until limp. Reduce heat to low.

Stir in the stock, wine, and brown sugar and cook, uncovered, stirring often, for about 45 minutes to 1 hour, until the liquid has evaporated and the leeks are golden brown.

While the leeks are cooking, heat the oven again to 400°F.

Scrub the potatoes and cut them into ⅓-inch-thick slices. Trim a sliver off of the four corners of each slice until they vaguely resemble stop signs. Discard the slivers.

Roast the potatoes on a lightly oiled baking sheet for 20 minutes, then remove from the oven and reduce the oven temperature to 350°F.

ASSEMBLE THE TART

When the leeks are done, remove them from the heat and cool for around 10 minutes. Spoon the cooled mixture into the prepared crust and spread it evenly across the bottom.

In a small bowl, whisk the eggs and cream with a pinch of salt to blend thoroughly. Pour the mixture evenly over the leeks, then sprinkle with the thyme.

Cover the top evenly with the potato slices, cutting them as needed to fill in any blank spots around the sides. Grind a few turns of pepper over the top of the potatoes.

Whisk the egg yolk and water in a small bowl, then use a pastry brush to brush the wash over the edges of the crust.

Set the pie pan on a rimmed baking sheet and bake in the 350°F oven for 45 minutes, until the crust is lightly browned and the filling is set.

Cool at least 20 minutes before serving.

GUEST RECIPE

Tricia Martin www.eatingisart.com

Tricia Martin lives at the intersection of food and art. An art director, photographer, and designer, she seamlessly melds edible and aesthetic worlds into projects for print, web, film, and experiential events. Tricia is also the creator of Pietopia, a national event that asks people to consider what their life would taste like if it were a pie. When she provided her spring–themed open–top Strawberry Pie recipe, Tricia had this to say about her pie's crust: "The piecrust recipe I use is from a dear, dear woman, Charlotte Arnette, who is also making the pies for my wedding. It is easy to make, easy to work with, and simply cannot be beat. I get a perfect crust every time I make it, which is hard to do with pie dough! Charlotte and her crust are sheer magic."

STRAWBERRY PIE

Makes: One 9-inch pie

YOU WILL NEED

9-inch pie pan

CRUST FOR ONE DOUBLE CRUST PIE

- ½ cup (1 stick) unsalted butter
- ½ cup shortening (I like to use a nonhydrognated shortening)
- 2½ cups all-purpose flour
- 2 tablespoons granulated sugar
- ½ teaspoon salt
- 2 large egg yolks
- 4 tablespoons ice water
- 1 teaspoon white vinegar

FILLING

- 2½ cartons (16 ounces each) fresh or frozen strawberries (4 heaping cups)
- 3 tablespoons cornstarch, arrowroot powder, or kudzu powder
- 1 tablespoon water
- 2 teaspoons pure vanilla extract
- ¼ cup (packed) brown sugar

PREPARE THE CRUST

Beat together the butter and shortening in a small bowl until smooth and creamy; chill until firm.

Sift together the flour, sugar, and salt into a medium bowl. Using a fork or pastry blender, cut the chilled butter and shortening into the dry ingredients until the mixture has a consistent texture.

Mix the egg yolks, ice water, and vinegar in a small bowl. Carefully stir the egg mixture into the flour/shortening mixture only until you can form the dough into a ball. (It's very important not to "overdo" mixing the liquid into the dry ingredients.) Form into a single ball for a one-crust pie. Refrigerate about 1 hour.

Preheat the oven to 450°F.

Roll out the chilled dough and press it into the 9–inch pie pan. Press parchment paper or aluminum foil into the crust and weigh the crust down with dried beans.

Bake the crust 15 minutes, then remove from the oven, leaving the oven on and reducing the temperature to 375°F.

Remove the beans and parchment paper, and prick the crust with a fork to allow steam to escape. Let the crust cool.

PREPARE THE FILLING

Wash and prepare the strawberries. Cut their tops off, cut them in half, then cut those halves again so you have fourths.

Put the cornstarch, arrow root, or kudzu into a small bowl with the tablespoon of water and let dissolve. You may need to stir it a little to help it along.

Toss the strawberries with the vanilla, sugar, and cornstarch/ arrow root/kudzu mixture and set aside. For a deeper, more intense strawberry flavor, allow the strawberries to mingle with the sugar and vanilla before you bake it.

ASSEMBLE THE PIE

Fill the cooled crust with the strawberry mixture. Place strips of aluminum foil approximately 2 inches wide to cover the edges of the piecrust so they do not brown to dark, inedible bits. Place the entire pie on a baking sheet to protect the oven from spillage; this pie is known to be juicy!

Bake at 375°F for 30 minutes, then reduce the temperature to 350°F and bake approximately 30 additional minutes.

This piecrust freezes well. Go ahead and double the batch so you can whip up another pie in no time! Simply wrap the extra dough in plastic wrap, then again in foil, and use within the month.

Beatrice Peltre www.latartinegourmande.com

Beatrice Peltre is fully immersed in the world of food. A cookbook author, food writer, food stylist and photographer, and recipe developer, Bea is a regular presence in international newspapers, French TV (she's a Boston-based transplanted Frenchwoman), and a number of cookbooks. She's also well-known for her beautiful, prize-winning blog La Tartine Gourmande, where she offers up stunning images of her food travels and seasonally based recipes. For spring, Bea is sharing her recipe for a delectable tart laden with seasonal goodies.

GLUTEN-FREE WATERCRESS, APPENZELLER CHEESE, AND SMOKED SALMON TART *Makes: One 11-inch tart or four 5-inch tartlets*

YOU WILL NEED

One 11-inch tart pan or four 5-inch tartlet pans

BUCKWHEAT AND MILLET CRUST

- ½ cup buckwheat flour
- ½ cup millet flour
- ½ cup white rice flour
- ½ cup quinoa flakes
- ½ teaspoon sea salt
- ¼ teaspoon xantham gum
- 3½ ounces (100 g) cold unsalted butter, diced
- 1 large egg
- 3 to 4 tablespoons cold water

FILLING

- 3½ ounces (100 g) watercress
  Sea salt
- ¼ cup plus 2 tablespoons crème fraîche
- 2 tablespoons olive oil
- 1 leek, white part only, finely chopped
- ½ red onion, finely chopped
- 1 teaspoon ground coriander
  Leaves from 3 twigs of lemon thyme
- 3 large eggs
- ¾ cup whole milk
  Freshly ground black pepper, to taste
- 1¾ ounces (50 g) Appenzeller cheese, finely grated
- 1¾ ounces (50 g) wild smoked sockeye salmon, finely diced

PREPARE THE CRUST

In the bowl of a food processor fitted with a dough blade, use the pulse function to combine the flours, quinoa flakes, salt, and xantham gum.

Add the butter and pulse until all is incorporated and the texture is crumbly. Do the same when adding the egg.

Add the water, one tablespoon at a time, and continue to pulse to combine all the ingredients. You have added enough water when the dough detaches from the bowl.

Wrap in plastic film and refrigerate for a minimum of an hour. Bring back to room temperature before using.

PREPARE THE FILLING

Blanch the watercress in a large volume of salted water for one minute. Rinse under cold water and squeeze excess water out.

Place in the bowl of a food processor with 2 tablespoons crème fraîche. Finely purée, and set aside in a large bowl.

In a sauté pan, warm the oil. Add the leek, onion, ground coriander, and lemon thyme. Cook, stirring without browning, for 5 minutes, until soft.

Transfer to the bowl containing the watercress and mix well; set aside.

In another bowl, beat the eggs with the milk and cup crème fraîche. Season with salt and pepper to taste and add the cheese and salmon. Add this mixture to the watercress mixture.

ASSEMBLE THE TART

Preheat the oven to 400°F.

Flour your working surface generously and roll out the dough to the size of the mold you want to use (for one 11-inch tart or four 5-inch tartlet molds). Make small holes with a fork in the bottom of the tart dough.

Add the filling and bake the tart or tartlets for 35 minutes, or until set and lightly browned.

Let cool for 5 minutes before slicing. Enjoy with a side salad.

Appenzeller is a hard cow's milk cheese made with raw milk and produced in the Appenzell region of northeastern Switzerland. Its taste is distinctive and pronounced. The cheese obtains its incomparable, delectable taste from being rubbed in a white wine and herb-based brine many times. You could substitute Emmenthal or Gruyère, or even Comté cheese, if Appenzeller is unavailable.

Gluten-Free Watercress, Appenzeller Cheese, and Smoked Salmon Tart

SUMMER

Long, languid days. Fireflies. Impromptu picnics and informal gatherings. Time spent sea-, pool-, or lakeside, thumbing through summer reads. This is the season of bountiful harvests and time spent outdoors. Pies made during the months of summer showcase juicy, fragrant offerings. From heavy, vine-ripened tomatoes to ambrosial peaches, summer's specimens make for perfect pie baking.

BASIL * BLACKBERRIES * BLUEBERRIES
CHERRIES (SWEET & SOUR) * CORN * EGGPLANT
MINT * NECTARINES * PEACHES
PEPPERS (SWEET AND HOT) * PLUMS
RASPBERRIES * TOMATOES
YELLOW SQUASH * ZUCCHINI

LATTICE-TOP TRIPLE BERRY PIE

Just as stunning to behold as it is delicious to consume, this pie makes use of three of summer's finest fruits: blackberries, blueberries, and raspberries. The lattice top comes together quickly, so don't be daunted by it. If you lack a pastry wheel, a pizza wheel makes a great stand-in. *Makes: One 9-inch pie*

YOU WILL NEED

- 1 recipe Basic Pie Dough (page 21)
- 9-inch pie pan

FILLING

- 3 cups blueberries
- 1½ cups blackberries
- 1½ cups raspberries
- ¾ cup granulated sugar
- ⅓ cup arrowroot powder or cornstarch
- 1 teaspoon ground ginger
- 1 teaspoon ground cinnamon
- Pinch of sea salt

EGG WASH

- 1 large egg yolk
- 1 tablespoon cold water
- 2 tablespoons turbinado sugar or other coarse sugar, for topping

PREPARE THE CRUST

Remove one dough disk from the refrigerator. Roll the dough out on a lightly floured surface and fit it into the 9-inch pie pan. Trim the crust overhang to 1 inch, then place the crust in the refrigerator while you prepare the filling.

PREPARE THE FILLING

Combine all the ingredients for the filling in a medium-size bowl. Stir with a large spoon to mix well, mashing the berries gently with the back of the spoon to release their juices. Cover the bowl with a kitchen cloth and leave to sit for 15 minutes.

Pour the mixed berry filling into the chilled crust.

ASSEMBLE THE PIE

Roll the remaining dough disk into a 12-inch circle. Using a pastry wheel, cut twelve 1-inch wide strips of dough. (I like to use the fluted edge of the pastry wheel, but you can use the smooth wheel, if you prefer.)

Arrange the lattice strips over the pie filling in alternating rows, weaving six strips horizontally and six vertically (see page 31 for detailed latticing instructions.) Trim the lattice strips to a 1-inch overhang and tuck the top and bottom overhangs under the bottom crust. Crimp the edges decoratively as desired.

Whisk the egg yolk and water in a small bowl, then use a pastry brush to brush the wash over the lattice and edges of the crust. Sprinkle the turbinado or other coarse sugar over the pie.

Place the pie in the refrigerator for at least 20 minutes.

Meanwhile, preheat the oven to 425°F.

Transfer the pie pan to a rimmed baking sheet lined with parchment paper or aluminum foil to catch overflow juices. Bake for 15 minutes.

Reduce the oven temperature to 375°F and bake an additional 35 minutes, until the crust is golden and juices are bubbling in the center of the pie.

Cool at least 4 hours before serving.

VARIATION: Trade 1 teaspoon of ground allspice for the ground ginger and cinnamon.

CHERRY AND VANILLA POT PIE

Cherries are one of summer's finest rewards. In this sweet version of a pot pie, I've partnered the crimson orbs with vanilla and added sliced almonds to the crust for a bit of crunch. Though you might be tempted to scoop yourself a serving of this as soon as it's out of the oven, hold out and give it plenty of time to cool. As it rests, the juices will gel, giving the pie substance and body. And, while I'm offering suggestions, I'd highly encourage the addition of a scoop of vanilla ice cream or whipped cream. They'll provide the figurative "cherry on top" of your cherry-studded delicacy! *Makes: One 8 x 8-inch pie*

YOU WILL NEED

- ½ recipe Basic Pie Dough (page 21)
-    8 x 8-inch baking dish or 9-inch deep-dish pie plate

FILLING

- 1 vanilla bean
- 3 pounds sweet cherries, pitted
- 3 tablespoons arrowroot powder or cornstarch
- ½ cup granulated sugar
- ½ teaspoon sea salt

EGG WASH

- 1 large egg yolk
- 1 tablespoon cold water

TOPPING

- 1 tablespoon turbinado sugar or other coarse sugar
- ¼ cup sliced almonds

Preheat the oven to 375°F. Butter the baking dish or pie plate. Set aside.

PREPARE THE CRUST

Remove the chilled pie dough from the refrigerator and roll it out into a 12-inch circle on a lightly floured surface. Transfer the dough to a large cookie sheet and refrigerate while you prepare the filling.

PREPARE THE FILLING

Slice the vanilla bean open. Using the tip of a paring knife, scrape out the seeds inside.

Combine the seeds with the cherries, arrowroot or cornstarch, sugar, and salt in a medium-size bowl. Stir together with a large spoon to mix well, mashing the cherries gently with the back of the spoon to release their juices. Cover the bowl with a kitchen cloth and leave to sit for 15 minutes.

ASSEMBLE THE PIE

Pour the cherry mixture into the prepared pan.

Cover with the chilled pie dough and trim to a 1-inch overhang. Fold the dough overhang over on the edges of the dish and crimp decoratively as desired.

Whisk the egg and water in a small bowl, then use a pastry brush to brush the wash over the crust. Cut four to six 2-inch slits in the crust, creating steam vents.

Sprinkle the turbinado sugar evenly over the surface of the pie and bake for 20 minutes. Scatter the sliced almonds over the crust and bake an additional 20 minutes, until the crust is golden brown and the almond slices are toasted.

Cool at least 1 hour before serving.

BLACKBERRY SONKER WITH "DIP"

The "sonker" is a type of deep-dish cobbler-like pie native to North Carolina, the state in which I live. It makes the use of whatever fruit is abundant and in season at the time of baking. Sonkers are traditionally served with "dip," a simple custard-like sauce. Historically, these types of pie are baked in large quantities to feed all of the workers on a farm. If you'd like to make a larger quantity, simply double all of the ingredient amounts and bake in a 13 x 9-inch baking dish.

Makes: One 10-inch skillet pie

YOU WILL NEED

10-inch skillet or 9-inch pie pan

FILLING

4½ half-pints blackberries (6 ounces each)

1 cup granulated sugar

¼ cup arrowroot powder or cornstarch

2 tablespoons all-purpose flour

1 teaspoon ground cinnamon

BISCUIT TOPPING

1 cup all-purpose flour

1 teaspoon baking powder

¼ teaspoon baking soda

¼ teaspoon sea salt

3 tablespoons unsalted butter, cubed

¾ cup buttermilk

3 tablespoons unsalted butter, melted

DIP

2 cups whole milk

½ cup granulated sugar

1 tablespoon arrowroot powder or cornstarch

1 teaspoon vanilla extract

Preheat the oven to 425°F. Butter the 10-inch skillet or 9-inch pie pan and set aside.

PREPARE THE FILLING

Combine all the ingredients for the filling in a medium-size bowl. Stir until the dry ingredients are thoroughly mixed and the berries are well coated.

Cover the bowl with a kitchen cloth and set aside for 15 minutes.

PREPARE THE BISCUIT TOPPING

Combine the flour, baking powder, baking soda, and salt in a medium-sized bowl.

Using a pastry blender or fork, cut in the butter cubes until the mixture is crumbly and the size of peas or smaller

Create a well in the center of the mixture. Pour in the buttermilk, and using a large spoon, gently incorporate just until all the dry ingredients are moistened. The mixture will look quite wet at this point, but that's fine.

PREPARE THE DIP

Heat the milk in a medium-size saucepan over medium heat. Bring to a gentle boil.

Whisk the sugar and starch in a small bowl to mix well, then add to the milk along with the vanilla extract, stirring until thoroughly blended and smooth.

Reduce the heat under the saucepan to a gentle simmer and cook, uncovered, 15 to 20 minutes until the mixture is reduced by half.

Remove from the heat and transfer the dip to a pourable container. Cover and set aside while the sonker bakes.

ASSEMBLE THE SONKER

Place the blackberry mixture in the prepared skillet.

Using a large spoon, dollop the surface of the blackberries with the biscuit topping, aiming for mounds of about 3 tablespoons of batter. You needn't be terribly specific on the biscuit amounts; as long as the surface is dotted with reasonably similar biscuit mounds, you're in good shape.

Pour the melted butter over the biscuit topping and bake for 15 minutes. Reduce the oven temperature to 350°F and continue baking an additional 30 minutes.

Cool at least 30 minutes, then, just before serving, drizzle each portion with several tablespoons of dip.

VARIATION: To make a raspberry or peach sonker, follow the recipe above, substituting an equal amount of raspberries or 4 cups peeled, pitted, and thinly sliced peaches for the blackberries.

PEACHES AND CREAM CRUMBLE-TOP PIE

"The best peach pie I have ever eaten" was the reply given by two friends of mine after eating this pie. They should know, too, both having been born and raised in the southeastern U.S., where peach pie is consumed on a near weekly basis come summertime. A custard base cradles a crunchy, buttery, spicy topping. The addition of almond extract to the filling really takes the flavor profile of this pie to the next level. *One 9-inch deep-dish pie*

YOU WILL NEED

½ recipe Basic Pie Dough (page 21)

A 9-inch deep-dish pie plate

CRUMBLE TOPPING

½ cup pecans, toasted and chopped (to toast, bake at 275°F for 4 to 5 minutes)

½ cup (packed) dark brown sugar

½ cup all-purpose flour

4 tablespoons (½ stick) butter

2 teaspoons ground cinnamon

FILLING

3 large eggs plus 2 large egg yolks

½ cup sour cream

¼ cup all-purpose flour

½ cup granulated sugar

1 teaspoon almond extract

2 pounds peaches, peeled, pitted and sliced into ½-inch slices

Preheat the oven to 400°F.

PREPARE THE CRUST

Roll out the dough on a lightly floured surface and fit it into a 9-inch deep-dish pie plate. Trim the crust overhang to 1 inch and crimp the edges decoratively. Prick the bottom of the crust 6 or 7 times with a fork, then place the crust in the refrigerator for 15 minutes.

Line the crust with parchment paper and fill it with dried beans or pie weights. Bake 10 minutes, then remove it from the oven, leaving the oven on and reducing the temperature to 375°F.

Remove the dried beans or pie weights and parchment paper from the crust, and cool it completely before filling.

PREPARE THE CRUMBLE TOPPING

Combine all the topping ingredients in a medium-size bowl. Using your hands, mix everything together until the butter is well incorporated and the mixture forms pea-size crumbles.

Cover the bowl with a kitchen cloth and place in the refrigerator to chill until ready to use.

PREPARE THE FILLING

Whisk together the eggs and egg yolks, sour cream, flour, sugar, and almond extract in another medium-size bowl.

ASSEMBLE THE PIE

Arrange the peach slices over the bottom of the cooled crust. Pour the filling over the peach slices. Set the pie pan on a rimmed baking sheet and bake in the 375°F oven for 35 minutes.

Remove the pie from the oven, leaving the oven on.

Sprinkle the chilled crumble topping evenly over the custard filling, then return the pie to the oven to bake an additional 15 minutes, until the crumble is golden brown.

Cool at least one hour before serving.

SUMMER

Peaches and Cream Crumble-Top Pie

BLUEBERRY REFRIGERATOR PIE

Refrigerator pies are ideal for those dog days of summer when it's simply too darn hot to turn on the oven. Aside from a short stint in the oven to pre-bake the crust, this pie requires no time in the oven whatsoever. The berries are first cooked down into a compote and then blended with cream and ricotta cheeses, creating an almost surreal purple hue. Studded with fresh berries on top, this pie is cool, creamy, and gorgeous. *Makes: One 9-inch deep-dish pie*

YOU WILL NEED

Graham Cracker Crust (page 23)

FILLING

- 1 tablespoon unsalted butter
- 1 pint blueberries
- ½ cup granulated sugar
- 2 tablespoons arrowroot powder or cornstarch
- 1 tablespoon lemon juice
- Grated zest of one lemon
- 8 ounces cream cheese, at room temperature
- 2 cups ricotta cheese, at room temperature

TOPPING

½ pint blueberries

PREPARE THE FILLING

Melt the butter in a medium-size saucepan. Add the blueberries and cook over medium heat for 5 minutes, until the berries begin to release their juices.

Mix together the sugar and starch in a small bowl. Stir into the blueberry mixture, then add the lemon juice and zest and cook 5 minutes longer, until the mixture thickens and becomes "jammy."

Remove from the heat and stir in the cream cheese and ricotta.

Transfer the mixture to a food processor or blender and puree for about one minute, until the mixture is smooth and creamy

ASSEMBLE THE PIE

Pour the blueberry and cheese mixture into the prepared crust. Arrange the half-pint of blueberries evenly over the surface of the pie, then refrigerate the pie for at least 8 hours or overnight. Serve chilled.

NECTARINE AND LAVENDER CROSTATA

Crostata is the Italian term for a free-form pie, similar to the French galette. In this version, ripe nectarines and fragrant lavender buds are partnered up. The result is a lovely, light, slightly tart yet gently floral dessert, perfect for when you want just a hint of sweetness on a hot summer day. This would be heavenly dolloped with fresh whipped cream. *Makes: 6 to 8 servings*

YOU WILL NEED

- ½ recipe Basic Pie Dough (page 21)
- Large un-rimmed baking sheet

FILLING

- 2 pounds nectarines, pitted and thinly sliced
- 3 tablespoons arrowroot powder or cornstarch
- ½ cup granulated sugar
- 1 tablespoon lavender buds, fresh or dried
- 1 teaspoon vanilla extract
- Pinch of sea salt
- 2 tablespoons unsalted butter, diced, for dotting the filling

EGG WASH

- 1 large egg yolk
- 1 tablespoon cold water

Preheat the oven to 375°F.

PREPARE THE CRUST

Remove the chilled pie dough from the refrigerator and roll it out into a 12-inch circle on a lightly floured surface. Transfer the dough to a large un-rimmed baking sheet and refrigerate while you prepare the filling.

PREPARE THE FILLING

Combine all the ingredients for the filling in a medium-size bowl. Stir until the ingredients are fully combined and the nectarine slices are well coated.

ASSEMBLE THE CROSTATA

Arrange the nectarine mixture evenly in concentric circles on top of the chilled pie dough, leaving a 2-inch border all around.

Dot the surface of the crostata with the diced butter and fold the pastry border up over the filling, overlapping the edges and pressing the folds together every few inches.

Whisk the egg yolk and water in a small bowl, then use a pastry brush to brush the wash over the folded edges of the crust.

Bake 30 minutes, until the crust is golden and the filling bubbles.

Cool at least 30 minutes before serving.

PEACH AND PLUM TART WITH MINT WALNUT PESTO

I adore the stone fruits of summer. Nectarines, peaches, and plums are a pie-maker's dream, with their fragrance, juiciness, and gem-like beauty. This tart uses another summer crop: fresh mint. This, with the addition of walnuts, renders a sweet pesto. *Makes: One 11-inch tart*

YOU WILL NEED

- ½ recipe Basic Pie Dough (page 21)
- 11-inch tart pan with removable bottom

FRUIT FILLING

- 1 pound peaches, peeled, pitted, and sliced ½ inch thick
- 1 pound plums, pitted and sliced ½ inch thick
- ⅔ cup (packed) light brown sugar
- 2 tablespoons arrowroot powder or cornstarch

MINT PESTO

- 2 cups walnuts
- ¼ cup (packed) light brown sugar
- ¼ cup olive oil
- ¼ cup chopped fresh mint
- 1 teaspoon ground nutmeg
- 1 teaspoon sea salt

TOPPING

- 1 tablespoon (packed) light brown sugar

Preheat the oven to 400°F.

PREPARE THE CRUST

Roll out the dough on a lightly floured surface and fit it into the tart pan. Trim the overhang to 1 inch, then fold it inside the tart pan, pressing it against the pan's fluted sides. Prick the bottom of the crust 6 or 7 times with a fork, then place the crust in the refrigerator for 15 minutes.

Line the crust with parchment paper and fill it with dried beans or pie weights. Bake 10 to 12 minutes, then remove from the oven, leaving the oven on and reducing the temperature to 375°F.

Remove the dried beans or pie weights and parchment paper from the crust, and cool it completely before filling.

PREPARE THE FRUIT FILLING

Combine all the ingredients for the fruit filling in a medium-size bowl. Stir with a large spoon until the fruit is fully coated with sugar and starch

Cover the bowl with a kitchen cloth and set aside while you prepare the mint pesto.

PREPARE THE MINT PESTO

Place all of the pesto ingredients in a food processor and puree until a paste is formed, about 1 to 2 minutes.

ASSEMBLE THE TART

Spread the pesto evenly across the bottom of the tart crust. Top with alternating slices of the peach and plum mixture, arranging the fruits in concentric circles. Sprinkle the brown sugar evenly over the filling.

Set the tart pan on a rimmed baking sheet and bake in the 375°F oven for 40 to 45 minutes, until the fruit becomes juicy and the brown sugar topping turns golden brown.

Cool at least 30 minutes before serving, first removing the sides of the pan.

VARIATION: Substitute pecans for the walnuts in the pesto.

RASPBERRY RAMEKIN MINI PIES

Sometimes you only want a little bit of pie. Or, on occasion, you need individualized, standout, noteworthy portions of pie, perhaps for a dinner party or bridal shower. In such cases, this is the summer pie you'll want to serve. The crusts are placed in small ramekins suitable for baking and then filled with a "not-for-the-faint-of-tart" raspberry and wine compote. The sides of the crust rise up above the filling, providing the perfect "cradle" for a scoop of ice cream (I suggest vanilla or butter pecan). *Makes: 8 servings*

YOU WILL NEED:

- ½ recipe Basic Pie Dough (page 21)
- 5-inch circular cookie cutter
- 8 ramekins, 3-inch size

FILLING:

- 1 tablespoon unsalted butter
- 4 half-pints raspberries (6 ounces each)
- 1 cup sparkling or white wine
- ½ cup granulated sugar
- 2 tablespoons arrowroot powder or cornstarch

Ice cream (flavor of choice), for serving

Preheat the oven to 375°F.

PREPARE THE CRUSTS

Roll out the dough into a 12-inch circle. Using a 5-inch cookie cutter, cut out 8 dough rounds. Re-roll scraps as necessary.

Lightly butter the ramekins, then line each with a dough round, tucking the rounds snugly up against the bottom and sides of the ramekin. Place the crust-lined ramekins in the refrigerator while you prepare the filling.

PREPARE THE FILLING

Melt the butter in a medium-size saucepan. Add the raspberries and cook over medium heat for 5 minutes, until the berries begin to release their juices.

Add the wine and stir to fully incorporate.

Mix together the sugar and arrowroot or cornstarch in a small bowl and stir into the raspberry mixture. Simmer over medium-low heat 5 to 7 minutes, until the mixture thickens and becomes syrupy.

ASSEMBLE THE MINI PIES

Fill the crust in each ramekin with ¼ cup of raspberry filling, and bake at for 20 to 25 minutes, until the crusts have puffed up and the raspberry filling is bubbly.

Cool at least 30 minutes before serving.

Place a scoop of ice cream over each mini pie and serve immediately.

VARIATION: These mini pies can also be made with blackberries. Simply substitute an equal amount for the raspberries.

CLASSIC BLUEBERRY PIE

Is there any more iconic summertime dessert than a classic blueberry pie? My maternal grandmother, Nanny, once owned a U-Pick blueberry farm in southeastern Virginia. I think of her every time I'm near the fruits. Bursting with berries and kissed with lemon, this pie will become your go-to version of the beloved treat. Do give it plenty of cooling time, as it needs it in order to properly firm up inside. *Makes: One 9-inch pie.*

YOU WILL NEED

- 1 recipe Basic Pie Dough (page 21)
- 9-inch pie pan

FILLING

- 2 pounds (6 cups) blueberries
- ⅔ cup granulated sugar
- ⅓ cup arrowroot powder or cornstarch
- 1 tablespoon grated lemon zest
- 1 teaspoon ground cinnamon
- ½ teaspoon ground nutmeg
- Pinch of sea salt
- 2 tablespoons lemon juice

- 3 tablespoons unsalted butter, diced, for dotting the filling

EGG WASH

- 1 large egg yolk
- 1 tablespoon whole milk

PREPARE THE CRUST

Remove one dough disk from the refrigerator and roll it out into a 12-inch circle. Fit it into the 9-inch pie pan and trim the crust overhang to 1 inch. Place the crust in the refrigerator while you prepare the filling.

PREPARE THE FILLING

Combine the blueberries, sugar, arrowroot or cornstarch, lemon zest, cinnamon, nutmeg, salt, and lemon juice in a medium-size bowl. Stir with a large spoon to mix well. Mash the berries gently with the back of the spoon to release their juices. Cover the bowl with a kitchen cloth and leave to sit for 15 minutes.

ASSEMBLE THE PIE

Roll the remaining dough disk to a 12-inch circle. Use a small pastry cutter to cut out decorative images in the dough. (I like to use a star-shaped cutter, but any design will work equally well; also see the tip.)

Pour the blueberry filling into the chilled crust and dot the surface with the diced butter.

Roll the top crust loosely over your rolling pin and unroll it over the filling in the pie pan, making sure it's centered. Trim the top crust overhang to 1 inch and tuck under the bottom crust overhang. Crimp the edges decoratively.

 Alternatively, you can simply cut four to six 2-inch slits in the crust, creating steam vents.

Whisk the egg yolk and milk in a small bowl, then use a pastry brush to brush the wash over the crust.

Place the pie in the refrigerator for at least 20 minutes.

Meanwhile, preheat the oven to 375°F.

Transfer the pie pan to a baking sheet lined with parchment paper or aluminum foil to catch overflow juices. Bake for 55 to 60 minutes, until the crust is golden and juices are bubbling in the center of the pie.

Cool at least 4 hours before serving.

VARIATION: Trade equal amounts of orange zest and juice for the lemon zest and juice.

FRIED GREEN TOMATO AND PIMENTO CHEESE TART

Living in the southeastern U.S. as I do, there are few dishes more regionally iconic than fried green tomatoes and pimento cheese. In this tart, I've taken the two and married them in a big savory, crispy union. Paired with a glass of chilled Pinot Grigio and a refreshing salad or bowl of gazpacho, you'll taste summer in every delicious bite. *Makes: One 11-inch tart (or 6 to 8 servings)*

YOU WILL NEED

- ½ recipe Basic Pie Dough (page 21)
- 11-inch tart pan with removable bottom

FRIED GREEN TOMATOES

- 2 large eggs
- 2 tablespoons whole milk
- 1 cup all-purpose flour
- 1 cup cornmeal
- 1 teaspoon granulated garlic
- 1 teaspoon paprika
- 1 teaspoon salt
- 2 medium-size green tomatoes, cut into slices ⅓-inch thick
- ¼ cup peanut oil

PIMENTO CHEESE

- 8 ounces cheddar cheese
- 1 roasted red pepper, diced
- 3 tablespoons mayonnaise
- 1 teaspoon paprika
- 1 slice bacon, cooked till crisp and crumbled (optional)

- 2 to 3 large basil leaves, for garnish

Preheat the oven to 400°F.

PREPARE THE CRUST

Roll out the dough on a lightly floured surface and fit it into the tart pan. Trim the overhang to 1 inch, then fold it inside the tart pan, pressing it against the pan's fluted sides. Prick the bottom of the crust 6 or 7 times with a fork, then place the crust in the refrigerator for 15 minutes.

Line the crust with parchment paper and fill it with dried beans or pie weights. Bake 10 to 12 minutes.

Remove the dried beans or pie weights and parchment paper from the crust, and cool it completely before filling.

PREPARE THE TOMATOES

Beat the eggs with the milk in a medium-size bowl.

In a separate bowl, whisk together the flour, cornmeal, granulated garlic, paprika, and salt.

Dip each tomato slice into the egg mixture, then in the flour mixture, repeating the process once. Place the dredged tomato slices on a platter as they are completed.

Heat the peanut oil in a medium-sized skillet over medium-high heat. Add the tomatoes and fry for about 5 minutes per side until lightly browned.

Remove the skillet from the heat and transfer the tomato slices with tongs to a paper towel–lined platter.

PREPARE THE PIMENTO CHEESE

Coarsely grate the cheddar cheese and combine with the red pepper, mayo, paprika, and bacon (if desired) in a food processor. Puree until smooth.

ASSEMBLE THE TART

Spoon the pimento cheese into the prepared crust, smoothing it level with a spatula.

Carefully place the largest fried green tomato slice in the center of the tart. Cut the rest of the slices in half and arrange the halves radiating out from the tomato in the center toward the edge.

Roll the basil leaves into a cylinder and cut into thin strips. Scatter this basil chiffonade evenly over the surface of the tart.

Serve chilled or at room temperature, removing the sides of the pan before serving.

RATATOUILLE AND POLENTA PIE

When I've got a bumper crop of fresh summer produce, my mind always goes to ratatouille. An easy way to use up loads of veggies all at once, it's the ideal summer dish. Here I've topped ratatouille with a generous portion of creamy polenta. Substantive enough to serve as an entrée, this pie would also partner well with some grilled summer sausages or chicken breasts. *Makes: 6 to 8 servings*

YOU WILL NEED

8 x 8-inch baking dish or 9-inch deep-dish pie plate

RATATOUILLE

1 pound eggplant, trimmed and cubed

8 ounces zucchini, trimmed and cubed

8 ounces yellow squash, trimmed and cubed

1 large sweet onion, diced

6 tablespoons olive oil

   Freshly ground black pepper, to taste

2 teaspoons sea salt

1 pound ripe tomatoes, cored and diced

½ cup red or rosé wine

1 tablespoon chopped fresh thyme

1 tablespoon chopped fresh parsley

   Hot pepper sauce, to taste (optional)

POLENTA

3 cups water

½ teaspoon sea salt, plus more to taste

1 cup polenta (coarse-ground yellow cornmeal)

2 tablespoons unsalted butter

1 tablespoon chopped fresh thyme

1 tablespoon chopped fresh parsley

   Freshly ground black pepper, to taste

Lightly grease the baking dish or pie plate with olive oil and set aside.

Preheat the oven to 400°F.

PREPARE THE RATATOUILLE

In a large bowl, toss the eggplant, zucchini, yellow squash, and onion with 4 tablespoons of the olive oil, a few grinds of black pepper, and 1 teaspoon of the salt.

Arrange the vegetable mixture in an even layer on a rimmed baking sheet, top with the diced tomatoes, and roast in the preheated oven for 1 hour.

Remove from the oven and transfer the vegetable mixture to a large saucepan with the remaining 2 tablespoons olive oil.

Add the wine, thyme, parsley, the remaining 1 teaspoon salt, and a dash of hot pepper sauce, if desired.

Cook over medium-low heat for 10 minutes, stirring frequently, until the liquid has cooked off. Remove from the heat and set aside while preparing the polenta.

PREPARE THE POLENTA

Boil the water and salt in a medium-size saucepan over high heat.

Gradually stir in the polenta in a thin, steady stream. Reduce the heat and simmer, stirring frequently to prevent sticking, until the mixture is very thick, about 10 to 15 minutes.

Remove from the heat and stir in the butter, fresh herbs, salt, and pepper to taste. Set aside.

ASSEMBLE THE PIE

Heat the broiler.

Pour the vegetable mixture into the prepared dish. Spoon the polenta over the vegetables and level it off with a spatula.

Place under the broiler for 5 to 8 minutes, until the polenta is golden brown.

Cool at least 15 minutes before serving.

VARIATION: Swap equal amounts of marjoram and oregano for the thyme and parsley in both the ratatouille and the polenta.

CARAMELIZED ONION AND BLUE CHEESE GALETTE

Whether you're hosting a light summer brunch or twilight cocktails on the patio, this is the tart you will want to serve. The tanginess of the blue cheese offers the perfect foil to the onion's sweetness. Keep in mind that what initially appears to be a mound of onions will reduce considerably over the slow cooking time. What results is a heap of the creamiest, most savory onion compote imaginable! Slice the galette into small wedges for appetizer portions or pair with roasted salmon for a light meal. *Makes: 6 to 8 servings*

YOU WILL NEED

½ recipe Basic Pie Dough (page 21)

Large un-rimmed baking sheet

FILLING

3 pounds onions

3 tablespoons unsalted butter

1½ cups white or rosé wine

1 cup chicken, beef, or vegetable stock

¼ cup granulated sugar

½ cup crumbled blue cheese

EGG WASH

1 large egg yolk

1 tablespoon whole milk

PREPARE THE CRUST

Remove the chilled pie dough from the refrigerator and roll it out into a 12-inch circle on a lightly floured surface. Transfer the dough to a large un-rimmed baking sheet and refrigerate while you prepare the filling.

PREPARE THE FILLING

Peel the onions, cut them into rings, and then cut each of the rings in half. Melt the butter in a large saucepan over medium heat. Add the onions and cook 15 minutes, stirring every few minutes.

Add the wine, stock, and sugar to the pan and cook, stirring the mixture every 4 to 5 minutes, for the next 45 minutes to 1 hour, until there is no more liquid at the bottom of the pan.

Continue cooking the onion mixture an additional 15 to 30 minutes, until the edges of the onions start to brown in places.

At this point, preheat the oven to 350°F.

Remove the pan with the onions from the heat and let it cool several minutes.

ASSEMBLE THE PIE

Spoon the onion mixture evenly over the center of the chilled pie dough circle, leaving a 2-inch border all around. Sprinkle the blue cheese evenly over the filling.

Fold the pastry border up over the filling, overlapping the edges and pressing the folds together every few inches.

Whisk the egg yolk and milk in a small bowl, then use a pastry brush to brush the wash over the folded edges of the crust. Bake 30 minutes, until the crust is golden.

Cool at least 30 minutes before serving.

VARIATION: If you're not a fan of blue cheese's pungent flavor, swap it out for an equal amount of feta or goat cheese.

ROASTED CORN AND PEPPER PIE

Corn and peppers truly shine during the swelter of summer. I recall childhood summers spent at the ocean (or the "shore," as it's colloquially known in New Jersey) devouring ear after ear of fresh, hot, buttery Silver Queen corn with my father's family. Roasting the vegetables imparts a bit of smokiness. Equally delicious served warm or cold, this is the sort of pie you can eat morning, noon, or night! *Makes: One 9-inch pie (or 6 to 8 servings)*

YOU WILL NEED

½ recipe Basic Pie Dough (page 21)

9-inch pie pan

FILLING

Peanut oil for grilling

 6 ears corn, shucked

 1 red bell pepper, seeded and diced

 1 poblano pepper, seeded and diced

 1 jalapeño pepper, seeded and finely diced

 5 large eggs

 ¼ cup sour cream

 ¼ cup half and-half

 2 teaspoons sea salt

 1 teaspoon chipotle powder or chili powder

 4 ounces Mexican farmer's cheese or feta cheese, crumbled

Preheat the oven to 375°F.

TIP If using a barbecue grill, cook the peppers whole first, then seed and dice.

When cool enough to handle, cut the corn kernels off the cobs. Add to the peppers in the bowl.

PREPARE THE CRUST

Roll out the dough on a lightly floured surface and fit it into the 9-inch pie pan. Trim the crust overhang to 1 inch and crimp the edges decoratively. Place the crust in the refrigerator while you prepare the filling.

PREPARE THE FILLING

Over high heat, "grill" the corn ears in a skillet with a few tablespoons of peanut oil. Turn partially every minute or so for 10 minutes, until the corn is mostly browned and blackened in some spots. Alternatively, you can lightly blacken the corn on a barbecue grill.

Remove the corn to a platter to cool slightly. Add a bit more peanut oil to the skillet and similarly brown and blacken the diced peppers. Remove the peppers to a medium-size bowl.

In a separate bowl, combine the eggs, sour cream, half-and-half, salt, and chipotle powder. Whisk until thoroughly incorporated.

ASSEMBLE THE PIE

Fill the chilled crust with the corn and peppers, leveling the vegetables with a spatula. Pour the egg mixture over the vegetables and sprinkle with the cheese.

Set the pie pan on a rimmed baking sheet and bake for 45 minutes, until the filling is golden brown on top and the eggs are cooked and not wobbly in the center.

Cool at least 30 minutes before serving.

VARIATION: If you don't care for the heat present in poblano and jalapeño peppers, simply substitute green bell peppers.

Jessie Oleson www.cakespy.com

Jessie Oleson is a self-described covert cake operative. Her blog (which is also now a brick-and-mortar store in Seattle's Capitol Hill neighborhood) describes itself as a "Dessert Detective Agency dedicated to seeking the sweetness in everyday life." Such discoveries are made by interviewing fellow bakers and food artisans, seeking out delicious baked goods, reviewing other bakeries, and performing multiple baking experiments. In addition to her blog, Jessie's writing can be found on DailyCandy, Serious Eats, and Taste of Home, as well as in her book *Cakespy Presents: Sweet Treats for a Sugar-Filled Life*.

SALTWATER TAFFY PIE

Makes: One 9-inch pie

YOU WILL NEED

- ½ recipe Basic Pie Dough (page 21)
  9-inch pie pan

FILLING

- ¾ cup granulated sugar
- ⅓ cup all-purpose flour
- 1½ cups whole milk
- 4 large eggs, separated
- 4 tablespoons (½ stick) butter
- 2 teaspoons vanilla extract
- 30 taffy candies, unwrapped (about 15 for the filling and as many as you'd like to garnish)
- ¼ teaspoon cream of tartar
- ⅛ teaspoon salt

Preheat the oven to 400°F.

PREPARE THE CRUST

Roll out the dough on a lightly floured surface and fit it into the 9-inch pie pan. Trim the crust overhang to 1 inch and crimp the edges decoratively. Prick the bottom of the crust 6 or 7 times with a fork, then place the crust in the refrigerator for 15 minutes.

Line the crust with parchment paper and fill it with dried beans or pie weights. Bake 10 to 12 minutes.

Remove the crust from the oven, leaving the oven on and reducing the temperature to 325°F. Remove the dried beans or pie weights and parchment paper, and cool the crust completely before filling.

PREPARE THE FILLING

In a medium saucepan, mix cup of the sugar and the flour. Add the milk and stir until blended. Add the egg yolks and mix very well.

Cook over low heat, stirring constantly, until thickened—this was about 15 minutes in total for me.

Remove from the heat and stir in the butter, 1 teaspoon vanilla extract, and 15 or so taffy candies. They may make bright swirls in the filling, which is not necessarily pretty or appetizing. Power through it.

Cool the mixture.

ASSEMBLE THE PIE

Pour the filling into the prepared crust.

In a large bowl, beat the egg whites on high speed with an electric mixer until stiff but not yet glossy. Sprinkle the cream of tartar and salt on top, and beat lightly.

Slowly add the remaining cup sugar and 1 teaspoon vanilla, beating constantly until the meringue forms soft peaks and has a nice glossy sheen, kind of like the consistency of shaving cream.

Spread over the pie.

Bake in the 325°F oven for 8 to 12 minutes, or until lightly browned. I found that to brown evenly, it helped to shift the plate halfway through baking.

Remove from the oven and let cool on a wire rack.

Once cool, dot the top with extra taffy, if desired.

Refrigerate leftovers; be warned that the taffy colors will bleed after a day, so this pie is best enjoyed the same day made.

Amanda Soule   www.soulemama.com

Amanda Blake Soule is the force behind the immensely popular blog soulemama, where she details her adventures in homemaking, parenting, creativity and more. In addition to her blog, she has authored three books: *The Creative Family, Handmade Home*, and most recently, *The Rhythm of Family*, co-written with her husband, Stephen. Amanda lives on her farm in western Maine with her husband and their five children, where they endeavor "to live simply, close to the earth and to each other."

SUMMER FERN PIE

Makes: 6 to 8 servings

YOU WILL NEED

9- or 10-inch pie plate

CRUST

1 cup unbleached flour
1 cup whole-wheat flour
8 tablespoons (1 stick) cold unsalted butter, cut into small pieces
¼ to ½ cup cold whole milk (or water)

FILLING

1 cup fiddleheads, rinsed
Juice of ½ lemon
½ teaspoon coarse sea salt
3 large eggs
1½ cups whole milk
1 cup shredded Swiss cheese
½ cup shredded cheddar cheese
Salt and pepper, to taste
½ pound bacon, cooked and diced

Preheat the oven to 375°F.

PREPARE THE CRUST

To make the crust, combine the flours in a food processor. Add the butter pieces and process for 60 seconds.

While running the food processor, add the milk (or water) slowly until the dough begins to hold together (how much milk you need to add may vary for you). If making the pie later, form the dough into a ball, wrap in plastic, and chill.

When ready to make your pie, roll out the dough on a floured surface. Roll until it's large enough to fit your 9- or 10-inch pie pan.

Transfer to the pie pan, pressing it down to fit. Trim excess, and press the edges to form a rim.

PREPARE THE FILLING

Steam the fiddleheads until tender, about 10 minutes. Place the fiddleheads in a bowl and toss with the lemon juice and sea salt.

In a separate bowl, whisk the eggs, milk, and cheeses together. Season with salt and pepper. Set aside.

ASSEMBLE THE PIE

Spread the fiddleheads and diced bacon evenly over the bottom of the piecrust. Pour the cheese mixture over the fiddleheads and bacon.

Bake at 375°F for 35 to 40 minutes, until the pie is "set" and beginning to turn golden (but not brown).

Let the pie sit for 10 minutes before slicing and serving.

AUTUMN

Pumpkins on the vine and decorated on the porch.

Vibrant sunflowers. Apple trees burdened with ripe fruit. Butternut, acorn, and spaghetti squashes ready for harvest and storage. The return of cardigans and scarves. Warming hands around a campfire. Autumn heralds the turn towards shorter days and cooler nights. It's also one of the busiest seasons, with so very much to harvest and store and prep. The calm before the (winter) storm, as it were. For me, autumn is quite possibly the best season for making pies, as there is an absolute bounty of material to work with. Look to your garden, farmer's markets, and area grocers, see what inspires you, and fire up the oven!

APPLES * CABBAGE * CRANBERRIES * FENNEL
FIGS * KALE * PEARS * PECANS * POMEGRANATES
PUMPKINS * QUINCES * ROSEMARY * SAGE
WINTER SQUASHES

PEAR CROSTATA

Tossed with warming spices and nestled in a buttery crust, this pear crostata comes together with ease and seriously delivers on flavor. It's the ideal treat to cap off an autumn picnic or to bring to a weekend brunch. For a special evening treat, serve it with a bit of port or sparkling cider.

Makes: 6 to 8 servings

YOU WILL NEED

- ½ recipe Basic Pie Dough (page 21)
- Large un-rimmed baking sheet

FILLING

- ½ cup granulated sugar
- ¼ cup arrowroot powder or cornstarch
- 5 pears, peeled, cored, and cut into ½-inch slices
- ½ teaspoon ground cinnamon
- ½ teaspoon ground ginger
- ¼ teaspoon ground allspice
- ¼ teaspoon sea salt
- 1 tablespoon lemon juice
- Grated zest of one orange

- 1 tablespoon unsalted butter, diced, for dotting the filling

EGG WASH

- 1 large egg yolk
- 1 tablespoon cold water

Preheat the oven to 375°F.

PREPARE THE CRUST

Remove the chilled pie dough from the refrigerator and roll it out into a 12-inch circle on a lightly floured surface. Transfer the dough to a large un-rimmed baking sheet, then return it to the refrigerator to chill while you prepare the filling.

PREPARE THE FILLING

Combine the sugar and arrowroot in a medium-size bowl. Add the pear slices, spices, salt, lemon juice, and orange zest. Using either clean hands or a large spoon, toss all the ingredients together.

ASSEMBLE THE CROSTATA

Mound the pear mixture in the middle of the chilled crust. Gently spread the mixture out toward the edge of the pastry, leaving a 2-inch border all around.

Dot the surface of the crostata with the diced butter.

Fold the pastry border up over the filling, overlapping the edges and pressing the folds together every few inches.

Whisk the egg yolk and water in a small bowl, then use a pastry brush to brush the wash over the folded edges of the crust. Bake for 30 to 35 minutes, until the crust is golden and the filling is bubbly in the center.

Cool the crostata at least 30 minutes before serving.

VARIATION: For an apple offering, swap an equal amount of apples for the pears.

ROSEMARY BOURBON SWEET POTATO PIE

I don't know about you, but I like my sweet potato pie served up with a bit of rosemary. The resinous, earthy flavor pairs expertly with the potatoes' inherent sweetness. Bourbon imparts an unexpected, subtle element of smokiness. Serve this up at Thanksgiving or for any autumn soiree, and watch it disappear! *Makes: One 9-inch pie*

YOU WILL NEED

½ recipe Basic Pie Dough (page 21)

9-inch pie pan

PECAN TOPPING

2 tablespoons unsalted butter

1 cup pecan halves

¼ cup maple syrup

1 tablespoon bourbon

1 teaspoon sea salt

FILLING

3 pounds sweet potatoes

4 large eggs, separated

1 cup heavy cream

4 tablespoons (½ stick) unsalted butter, cubed

½ cup bourbon

¼ cup maple syrup

¼ cup (packed) light brown sugar

2 tablespoons finely chopped fresh rosemary

1 teaspoon sea salt

½ teaspoon ground allspice

½ teaspoon ground cinnamon

½ teaspoon ground nutmeg

EGG WASH

1 large egg yolk

1 tablespoon cold water

Preheat the oven to 400°F.

PREPARE THE CRUST

Roll out the dough on a lightly floured surface and fit it into the 9-inch pie pan. Trim the crust overhang to 1 inch and crimp the edges decoratively. Place the crust in the refrigerator while you prepare the topping and filling.

PREPARE THE PECAN TOPPING

Melt the butter in a medium-size saucepan over medium heat. Add the pecans, maple syrup, bourbon, and salt and cook, stirring occasionally, 4 to 5 minutes, until the mixture is thick and gooey.

Remove from the heat and set aside to cool.

PREPARE THE SWEET POTATOES

Prick the potatoes 3 or 4 times apiece with the tines of a kitchen fork.

Line a rimmed baking sheet with parchment paper. Place the potatoes on the baking sheet and bake for 1 hour.

Remove the potatoes from the oven, leaving the oven on and reducing the temperature to 350°F.

Let the potatoes stand 10 to 15 minutes, until cool enough to handle. Peel off the skins off and put the flesh in a large bowl. Mash with a potato masher until softened and smooth.

PREPARE THE REST OF THE FILLING

Using an electric mixer or a whisk, beat the egg whites in a medium-size bowl until billowy peaks form. Set aside.

Add the heavy cream and butter to the bowl containing the mashed sweet potatoes. Whisk until the butter melts and the cream is well incorporated, then whisk in the egg yolks until fully combined.

Place the bourbon in a medium-size saucepan. Bring to a boil over high heat and boil vigorously for 1 to 2 minutes, then stir in the maple syrup and brown sugar. Boil 2 to 3 minutes longer, until the brown sugar melts.

Remove from the heat and pour into the potato mixture. Whisk until well combined. Add the rosemary, salt, allspice, cinnamon, and nutmeg and whisk to blend thoroughly.

Add the beaten egg whites to the potato mixture. Fold in gently with a spatula until the whites are fully incorporated.

ASSEMBLE THE PIE

Pour the filling into the chilled crust, using a spatula to distribute it evenly. Arrange the candied pecans decoratively over the filling in a pattern that you like—if you don't cover the entire pie, you get to eat the leftover pecans!

Whisk the egg yolk and water in a small bowl, then use a pastrybrush to brush the wash over the edges of the crust.

Bake in the 350°F oven for 1 hour, until the filling is set and doesn't jiggle when the pie pan is gently shaken.

Cool at least 50 to 60 minutes before serving, so the pie has time to set up and firm throughout.

CHAI SPICE APPLE PIE

I'm a devoted chai drinker. As soon as a cool breeze blows into my mountain cove, I begin brewing up pots of the spicy tea on a nearly daily basis. Here I've married the sweetness of apples—autumn's mascot fruit—with the warming heat of cardamom, cinnamon, ginger, fennel, pepper, and cloves. All are tossed in a bit of black tea and baked into spicy submission. The result is one that's destined to make a chai lover out of you, too. While delightful on its own, this pie is rendered sublime when partnered with cinnamon ice cream. *Makes: One 9-inch pie*

YOU WILL NEED

    1 recipe Basic Pie Dough (page 21)

    9-inch pie pan

CHAI SPICE BLEND

    1 teaspoon cardamom seeds or ground
       cardamom

    ½ teaspoon black tea

    ¼ teaspoon whole cloves

    ¼ teaspoon black peppercorns

    ¼ teaspoon fennel seeds

    1 teaspoon ground cinnamon

    ¼ teaspoon ground ginger

FILLING

    3 pounds apples, (I suggest Gala, Fuji, Pink
       Lady, Stayman, or Honeycrisp), peeled,
       cored, quartered, and cut into ½-inch-thick
       slices

    4 tablespoons all-purpose flour

    ¼ cup granulated sugar

    2 tablespoons lemon juice

    ½ teaspoon sea salt

    2 tablespoons unsalted butter, diced, for
       dotting the filling

EGG WASH

    1 large egg yolk

    1 tablespoon whole milk

TOPPING

    1 tablespoon turbinado sugar or other
       coarse sugar

    1 teaspoon ground cinnamon

Cinnamon ice cream, for serving (optional; see
the tip)

TIP To make cinnamon ice cream, combine 1
half-gallon vanilla ice cream, softened,
with 2 teaspoons ground cinnamon in a
large bowl. Stir with a large spoon to
incorporate the cinnamon into the ice
cream, then scrape the mixture back into
the ice cream container. Place in the
freezer until ready to serve with the pie.

PREPARE THE CRUST

Remove one dough disk from the refrigerator. Roll out the dough on
a lightly floured surface and fit it into a 9-inch pie pan. Trim the crust
overhang to 1 inch, then place the crust in the refrigerator while you
prepare the filling.

PREPARE THE CHAI SPICE BLEND

Using either a mortar and pestle or a spice or coffee grinder, grind
the cardamom seeds (if using), black tea, whole cloves, peppercorns,
and fennel seeds to a powder.

Pour the ground spices into a fine-mesh sieve placed over a small
bowl. Gently shake the sieve so all but the larger pieces fall through.
Discard the larger pieces left in the sieve.

To the freshly ground spices in the bowl, add the ground cardamom
(if using), cinnamon, and ginger. Whisk well to combine.

PREPARE THE FILLING

Combine all of the filling ingredients, including the chai spice blend,
in a medium-sized mixing bowl. Using either clean hands or a large
spoon, toss until all of the ingredients are fully combined and the
apple slices are evenly coated.

ASSEMBLE THE PIE

Pour the apple mixture into the prepared crust, mounding in the
center. Dot the surface with the diced butter.

Roll the remaining dough disk into a 12-inch circle. Use a small
pastry cutter to cut decorative images in the dough. (I like to use
a leaf-shaped, autumn-theme cutter, but any design will work
equally well.)

TIP Instead of cutting decorative images in the
dough, you can simply cut four to six 2-inch
slits in the crust to create steam vents.

Roll the top crust loosely over your rolling pin and unroll it
over the filling in the pie pan, making sure it's centered.
Trim the top crust overhang to 1 inch and tuck the edges
under the bottom crust overhang. Crimp the edges
decoratively.

Whisk the egg yolk and milk in a small bowl, then use a
pastry brush to brush the wash over the crust.

Place the pie in the refrigerator for 15 minutes.

Meanwhile, preheat the oven to 425°F.

Mix the coarse sugar and ground cinnamon in a small bowl
and sprinkle it evenly over the pie.

Place the pie on a baking sheet lined with parchment paper or aluminum foil to catch overflow juices and bake at for 20 minutes. Reduce the oven temperature to 375°F and continue baking for 30 to 35 minutes longer, until the crust is golden and juices are bubbling in the center of the pie.

Cool at least 1 hour before serving, accompanied, if desired but as recommended, with cinnamon ice cream.

VARIATION: For a pear version, swap an equal amount of pears for the apples.

GINGERSNAP PUMPKIN PIE WITH CANDIED PUMPKIN SEEDS

This modern take on the traditional pumpkin pie has a little something for everyone. A robust, no-holds-barred gingersnap crust for the spice lover, a creamy custard filling for the traditionalist, and candied pumpkin seeds on top for the person who likes a little crunch with their sweets. You can make this either in a standard 9-inch pie pan, or in a springform pan, which makes for a particularly pretty presentation, with the crust rising up to meet the bright orange filling.

Makes: One 9-inch pie

YOU WILL NEED

Gingersnap Crust (page 22)

FILLING

2 cups pumpkin purée (see the tip)

¾ cup (packed) light brown sugar

½ teaspoon ground cinnamon

½ teaspoon ground nutmeg

½ teaspoon ground ginger

1 teaspoon sea salt

¾ cup heavy cream

½ cup whole milk

2 large eggs, beaten

2 teaspoons vanilla extract

PUMPKIN SEED TOPPING

½ cup toasted pumpkin seeds (to toast, bake at 275°F for 4 to 5 minutes)

3 tablespoons unsalted butter, melted

2 tablespoons granulated sugar

2 tablespoons minced crystallized ginger

½ teaspoon sea salt

¼ teaspoons ground cloves

Preheat the oven to 350°F.

PREPARE THE FILLING

Combine all the filling ingredients in a medium-size bowl and whisk to blend well.

PREPARE THE PUMPKIN SEED TOPPING

Combine all the topping ingredients in a small bowl. Using a large spoon, stir until the pumpkin seeds are evenly coated with the butter, sugar, and spices.

ASSEMBLE THE PIE

Pour the filling into the prepared gingersnap crust and bake for 40 minutes.

Remove the pie from the oven, leaving the oven on. Sprinkle the pumpkin seed topping evenly over the pie, then return it to the oven and bake another 20 minutes, until the pumpkin seeds have browned slightly and the filling has set.

Cool at least 1 hour before serving.

VARIATION: Replace the pumpkin seeds with an equal amount of chopped pecans for a pecan praline topping.

For pumpkin purée, cut a 5- to 6-pound baking pumpkin in half. Place flesh side down on a rimmed baking sheet and roast at 425°F until the flesh has softened, about 45 to 50 minutes. Cool slightly, then remove the seeds, scoop the flesh out of the skin, and puree in a food processor until smooth. You can also simply use solid-pack canned pumpkin.

PUMPKIN TIRAMISÙ PIE

Tiramisù holds a special place in my heart. I used to work in a production kitchen where batches of it were created on a regular basis. Every time I eat it now, I'm taken back to fond memories spent with buttery hands, floured faces, and very, very dirty aprons. Add a bit of pumpkin puree (one of my most beloved things about autumn) to the dessert and this pie quickly climbs the ranks to all-time favorite. This recipe calls for pound cake in place of the customary ladyfingers, resulting in a more robust offering, fantastic for those chilly autumn days when a bit of stick-to-your-ribs noshing is in order. (You may end up with a few extra slices of pound cake after the pie is assembled. Enjoy them with an afternoon cup of tea!) *Makes: One 9-inch pie*

YOU WILL NEED

    9 x 5-inch loaf pan

    9-inch deep-dish pie plate

POUND CAKE

    4 large eggs, separated

    1 cup (2 sticks) butter, at room temperature

    1½ cups granulated sugar

    2 cups all-purpose flour

PUMPKIN FILLING

    ¾ cup heavy cream

    ¼ cup powdered sugar

    2 cups pumpkin purée (see the tip on page 147)

    ½ teaspoon ground cinnamon

    ½ teaspoon ground nutmeg

    ¼ teaspoon ground allspice

    ¼ teaspoon ground ginger

    ¼ teaspoon ground cloves

MASCARPONE FILLING:

    1 cup heavy cream

    3 tablespoons powdered sugar

    8 ounces mascarpone

COFFEE GLAZE

    ½ cup strong brewed coffee

    ¼ cup Kahlúa

Ground cinnamon and nutmeg for sprinkling (optional)

Preheat the oven to 350°F.

PREPARE THE POUND CAKE

Lightly butter the 9 x 5-inch loaf pan.

Using an electric mixer or a whisk, beat the egg whites in a medium-size bowl until light and billowy. Set aside.

In a separate bowl, using an electric mixer, cream the butter and sugar until light and fluffy, about 3 to 4 minutes.

Add the egg yolks, one at a time, beating well and scraping the bowl and beaters with a spatula after each addition.

Using a spatula, gently fold in the beaten egg whites until fully incorporated.

Add the flour, one cup at a time, scraping down the bowl and beaters after each addition.

Pour the batter into the prepared pan, using a spatula to spread the batter evenly.

Bake for 65 to 75 minutes, until the top is golden brown and a knife inserted into the center comes out clean.

Cool in the pan for 15 minutes, then remove from the pan and leave to cool on a rack an additional 15 minutes.

Cut the cooled pound cake lengthwise down the center, using a serrated knife. Then, cut crosswise into ½-inch pieces.

PREPARE THE PUMPKIN FILLING

Using an electric mixer or a whisk, beat the heavy cream and powered sugar in a medium-size bowl until billowy peaks form. By hand, gently stir in the pumpkin puree and spices, mixing until all the ingredients are fully incorporated into the whipped cream.

PREPARE THE MASCARPONE FILLING

Using an electric mixer or a whisk, beat the heavy cream and powered sugar in a medium-sized bowl until billowy peaks form. Add the mascarpone and beat until well incorporated into the whipped cream.

PREPARE THE COFFEE GLAZE

Combine the coffee and Kahlúa in a small bowl and stir to blend well.

ASSEMBLE THE TIRAMISÙ

Spread half the pumpkin filling evenly over the bottom of the deep-dish pie plate. Top the pumpkin filling with half of the pound cake slices, trimming them to fit the dish as necessary.

Next, drizzle half of the coffee glaze over the pound cake slices, then top them with an even layer of half of the mascarpone filling.

Repeat the entire process: pumpkin filling, pound cake slices, coffee glaze, and mascarpone filling. Then, if desired, sprinkle the pie with a little ground cinnamon and nutmeg.

Refrigerate the pie at least 1 hour before serving.

VARIATION: For an alcohol-free version, omit the Kahlúa and increase the coffee to ¾ cup.

APPLE CRÈME BRÛLÉE MINI PIES

The creamy, smokiness of crème brûlée is the perfect foil for the tart heat of gingered apples. Nestled into individual ramekins, these mini pies would be a stunning end note to an elegant dinner party, bridesmaid's luncheon, or autumn baby shower. *Makes: 8 servings*

YOU WILL NEED

½ recipe Basic Pie Dough (page 21)

5-inch circular cookie cutter

8 ramekins, 3-inch size

APPLE FILLING

3 tablespoons unsalted butter

2 medium-size apples, peeled, cored, and roughly chopped into ½-inch pieces

1 tablespoon lemon juice

1 tablespoon granulated sugar

½ teaspoon ground ginger

CUSTARD FILLING

8 large egg yolks

¼ cup granulated sugar

1½ cups heavy cream

TOPPING

½ cup granulated sugar

Preheat the oven to 400°F.

PREPARE THE CRUST

Roll out the dough on a lightly floured surface into a 12- to 14-inch circle. Using a 5-inch cookie cutter, cut out 8 rounds. You may have to reroll the dough scraps several times to cut out all of the rounds. Do so quickly, as the more the dough is rolled, the more it activates the gluten in the wheat, which can result in toughened dough.

Lightly butter the ramekins, then line each with a dough round, pressing the dough against the ramekin bottom and sides.

Cut out 8 small squares of parchment paper. Line each dough-lined ramekin with the parchment paper and fill each with dried beans or pie weights.

Place the ramekins on a rimmed baking sheet and chill in the refrigerator for at least 15 minutes.

Bake the ramekins on the baking sheet for 10 minutes, then remove from the oven, leaving the oven on and reducing the temperature to 375°F.

Cool the ramekins for about 10 minutes, then remove the pie weights and parchment paper.

Set the ramekins aside, still on the baking sheet, while you prepare the apple and custard fillings.

PREPARE THE APPLE FILLING

Melt the butter in a medium-size saucepan over medium-low heat. Add the apples and reduce the heat to low. Cook 8 to 10 minutes, stirring occasionally, until the apples have softened.

Add the lemon juice, sugar, and ginger. Cook 2 to 3 minutes, stirring until the mixture is bubbly and well combined.

Remove the saucepan from the heat and set aside to cool slightly while you prepare the custard filling.

PREPARE THE CUSTARD FILLING

Combine the egg yolks and sugar in a medium-size mixing bowl. Whisk until well blended.

Heat the cream in a small saucepan over medium heat, just until bubbles begin forming at the edge of the pan.

Remove the cream from the heat and drizzle it slowly into the egg yolk mixture, whisking constantly until fully blended.

ASSEMBLE THE MINI PIES

Place about 1 tablespoon of the apple filling in the crust in each ramekin, then pour in the custard filling to divide evenly.

Bake for 25 minutes, until the top of the custard has lightly browned and the filling has set.

Remove from the oven and cool the ramekins at least 30 minutes.

About 20 or 25 minutes before serving, sprinkle 1 tablespoon of the sugar over the filling in each ramekin.

Using either a crème brûlée torch or the highest broiler setting of your oven, brown the tops of each mini pie until the sugar darkens and bubbles. Set aside to cool at least 5 to 10 minutes before serving (this allows the sugar to harden, so that the surface will "crack" when tapped with a spoon).

FIGGY PUDDING PIE

When figs are in season, I consume them with abandon. Eaten straight from the tree, cooked into a delicious jam, or roasted and paired with custard, as here, figs can do no wrong, in my estimation. A slice of this pie would be sheer heaven when partnered with a hot toddy and enjoyed around a wood stove or fire ring. *Makes: One 9-inch pie*

YOU WILL NEED

- ½ recipe Basic Pie Dough (page 21)
- 9-inch deep-dish pie plate

ROASTED FIGS

- 1½ pounds fresh figs, stemmed and quartered
- 2 tablespoons olive oil
- 2 tablespoons honey
- ¼ teaspoon sea salt

CUSTARD FILLING

- 3 large eggs plus 2 large egg yolks
- 1 cup heavy cream
- ¾ cup granulated sugar
- 1 teaspoon ground nutmeg
- 1 teaspoon ground cinnamon
- ¼ teaspoon ground cloves
- ¼ teaspoon ground allspice
- 1 teaspoon vanilla extract

Preheat the oven to 400°F.

PREPARE THE CRUST

Roll out the dough on a lightly floured surface and fit it into a 9-inch deep-dish pie plate. Trim the crust overhang to 1 inch and crimp the edges decoratively. Prick the bottom of the crust 6 or 7 times with a fork, then place the crust in the refrigerator for at least 15 minutes.

Line the crust with parchment and fill it with pie weights or dried beans. Bake for 10 to 12 minutes, then remove from the oven, leaving the oven on but turning the setting to broil.

Remove the pie weights and parchment from the crust and cool it slightly before filling.

PREPARE THE ROASTED FIGS

Toss the quartered figs with the olive oil in a medium-size bowl.

Place flesh side up on a rimmed baking sheet and drizzle with the honey. Sprinkle evenly with the salt.

Broil the figs under high heat 8 to 10 minutes, until they become a bit crisp and slightly blackened at the edges.

Remove from the oven and set aside to cool slightly while you prepare the custard filling.

Adjust the oven setting to 350°F.

PREPARE THE CUSTARD FILLING

Whisk together the eggs and egg yolks in a medium-size bowl. Add the cream, sugar, spices, and vanilla and whisk to blend thoroughly.

ASSEMBLE THE PIE

Place the roasted figs evenly over the prepared piecrust. Pour the custard filling over the figs.

Bake in the 350°F oven for 1 hour, until the filling is set and doesn't jiggle when the pie pan is gently shaken.

Cool at least 1 hour before serving.

CRANBERRY MINCE TART

Without question my go-to Thanksgiving dessert, this tart showcases the best of what cranberries have to offer. While not for the "faint of tart," the fruit's inherent puckery-ness is tempered by the inclusion of raisins, currants, crystallized ginger, orange juice, and sugar. Don't be intimidated by the ingredient listing—the dish comes together very quickly. And do serve it with the orange whipped cream detailed below, as it even further balances the berries' "bite." *Makes: One 11-inch tart*

YOU WILL NEED

½ recipe Basic Pie Dough (page 21)

11-inch tart pan with removable bottom

ORANGE WHIPPED CREAM

1 cup heavy cream

3 tablespoons powdered sugar

½ teaspoon orange extract

FILLING

2 cups granulated sugar

½ cup water

½ cup orange juice

6 cups cranberries (two 12-ounce bags) (see the tip)

Grated zest of 1 orange

¼ cup arrowroot powder or cornstarch

1 cup pecans, chopped

½ cup dark raisins

½ cup golden raisins

¼ cup currants

2 tablespoons minced crystallized ginger

1 teaspoon ground cinnamon

½ teaspoon ground nutmeg

¼ teaspoon ground cloves

¼ teaspoon ground allspice

½ teaspoon sea salt

Preheat the oven to 400°F.

 TIP Fresh or frozen cranberries will work equally well here. If you go the frozen route, simply allow the cranberries to thaw overnight in the refrigerator before use.

PREPARE THE CRUST

Roll out the dough on a lightly floured surface and fit it into the tart pan. Trim the overhang to 1 inch, then fold it inside the tart pan, pressing it against the pan's fluted sides.

Prick the bottom of the crust 6 or 7 times with a fork, then place the crust in the refrigerator for 15 minutes.

Line the crust with parchment paper and fill it with dried beans or pie weights. Bake 10 to 12 minutes, then remove from the oven, leaving the oven on and reducing the temperature to 375°F.

Remove the dried beans or pie weights and parchment paper from the crust, and cool it slightly before filling.

PREPARE THE ORANGE WHIPPED CREAM

Combine the heavy cream, powdered sugar, and orange extract in a medium-size bowl. Using an electric mixer, beat at highest speed until billowy peaks form.

Transfer the whipped cream to a serving bowl and chill in the refrigerator until ready to serve with the pie.

PREPARE THE FILLING

Combine the sugar, water, and orange juice in a medium-size saucepan and heat, stirring, over medium-high heat until the sugar has completely dissolved.

Add the cranberries and orange zest and reduce the heat to medium. Cook, uncovered, 5 to 7 minutes, until some of the cranberries have popped and the liquid is gently simmering.

Remove from the heat and whisk in the arrowroot or cornstarch until fully incorporated into the cranberry mixture. Set aside.

Combine the pecans, dark raisins, golden raisins, currants, crystallized ginger, spices, and salt in a medium-size bowl. Stir to mix thoroughly.

Add the cranberry mixture to the bowl with the nuts and fruits, and stir again to mix thoroughly.

ASSEMBLE THE TART

Pour the filling into the prepared crust, using a spatula to spread it evenly. Bake in the 375°F oven for 25 minutes, until the crust edges are golden brown and the filling is set.

Cool at least 1 hour before serving with the orange whipped cream, and first removing the sides of the pan.

SALTED PECAN MINI TARTS

For the most part, I find that pecan pie typically falls on the cloyingly sweet side of the flavor spectrum. Here, I've captured the best the pie has to offer and packed it into tiny, delectable bites. Topped off with a few coarse sea salt granules, these might just become your new favorite way of eating pecan pie. They also make a fantastic offering to bring to a holiday cookie exchange (which I host every year—so much fun!). *Makes: 36 mini tarts*

YOU WILL NEED

½ recipe Basic Pie Dough (page 21)

2½-inch round biscuit or cookie cutter

Mini tart pans

FILLING

½ cup (packed) light brown sugar

2 tablespoons unsalted butter, melted

1 large egg

½ teaspoon vanilla extract

½ teaspoon ground nutmeg

¼ teaspoon sea salt

¾ cup pecans, chopped

A tablespoon or so of coarse sea salt, for sprinkling

PREPARE THE CRUST

Roll out the chilled dough on a lightly floured surface into a 12- or 14-inch circle. Cut out 36 rounds, using a 2½-inch round biscuit or cookie cutter. You may have to reroll the dough scraps several times to cut out all of the rounds. Do so quickly, as the more the dough is rolled, the more it activates the gluten in the wheat, which can result in toughened dough.

Place one dough round in each mini tart pan. Press the dough flat against the bottom and up the sides of the pan. Place each tart pan as it is prepared on one of two large baking sheets.

Put the baking pans with the mini tart pans in the refrigerator to chill for 20 minutes.

Meanwhile, preheat the oven to 325°F.

Bake the chilled mini tart crusts for 8 minutes.

Remove the baking sheets from the oven, leaving the oven on and raising the temperature to 375°F. Set the mini tart crusts aside to cool while you prepare the filling.

PREPARE THE FILLING

Combine the brown sugar, butter, egg, vanilla extract, nutmeg, and salt in a medium-size bowl. Whisk to blend thoroughly, then stir in the chopped pecans.

ASSEMBLE THE MINI TARTS

Spoon 1 teaspoon of the filling into each mini tart shell (see the tip), then sprinkle each with several granules of coarse sea salt.

Bake in the 375°F oven for 25 minutes, until the tops are lightly browned.

Cool the mini tarts at least 15 minutes before serving.

TIP A spoon with a pointed tip, such as a grapefruit spoon, is especially helpful when filling the mini tarts, as the tip will help guide the filling into the tiny tart shells.

ROASTED BEET AND APPLE PIE

Beets and apples were made for one another. Roasted together here and pureed with creamy cottage cheese, eggs, and horseradish, this pie screams "Autumn!" from the rooftops. Serve it with a bit of the horseradish cream detailed below for a creamy foil to the pie's earthy sweetness.

Makes: One 9-inch deep-dish pie

YOU WILL NEED

- ½ recipe Basic Pie Dough (page 21)
- 9-inch deep-dish pie plate

HORSERADISH CREAM

- 1 cup sour cream
- 1 teaspoon horseradish (see the tip)

FILLING

- 2 pounds beets, peeled and cubed
- 2 apples, peeled, cored, and quartered
- 1 to 2 tablespoons olive oil
- Freshly ground black pepper, to taste
- 1 pound small-curd cottage cheese
- 5 large eggs, beaten
- 2 tablespoons horseradish
- 3 tablespoons white wine vinegar
- 1 tablespoon chopped fresh chervil, tarragon, or parsley
- 2 teaspoons granulated sugar
- 1 teaspoon sea salt
- 1 teaspoon paprika

EGG WASH

- 1 large egg yolk
- 1 tablespoon cold water

Preheat the oven to 400°F.

 TIP Feel free to use either fresh or prepared horseradish. For every tablespoon of fresh horseradish, use 2 tablespoons prepared.

PREPARE THE CRUST

Roll out the dough on a lightly floured surface and fit it into the deep-dish pie plate. Trim the crust overhang to 1 inch and crimp the edges decoratively. Prick the bottom of the crust 6 to 7 times with a fork, then place the crust in the refrigerator for at least 15 minutes.

Line the crust with parchment paper and fill it with dried beans or pie weights. Bake for 10 to 12 minutes, then remove from the oven, leaving the oven on and reducing the heat to 375°F.

Remove the dried beans or pie weights and parchment paper from the crust, and cool it slightly before filling.

PREPARE THE HORSERADISH CREAM

Combine the sour cream and horseradish in a small bowl and stir to mix thoroughly. Cover and store in the refrigerator until ready to serve with the pie.

PREPARE THE FILLING

Toss the beets and apples with the olive oil on a rimmed baking sheet. Add several grinds of black pepper, then roast for 1 hour, turning the baking sheet halfway through.

Remove from the oven and let the beets and apples cool for 15 to 20 minutes.

Combine the roasted beets and apples with the remaining ingredients in a food processor. Puree until smooth, working in batches if necessary.

ASSEMBLE THE PIE

Pour the filling into the prepared crust.

Whisk the egg yolk and water in a small bowl, then use a pastry brush to brush the wash over the edges of the crust.

Bake the pie in the 375°F oven for 45 minutes, until the filling is set and doesn't jiggle when the pie plate is gently shaken.

Cool at least 30 minutes before serving, accompanied by the horseradish cream.

ROASTED BUTTERNUT SQUASH, CHEDDAR, AND SAGE GALETTE

Winter squashes are a bit of a misnomer, as they're actually harvested in late summer and dried, or "cured," for later use in autumn and beyond. Butternut squash truly shines in this galette. Its lovely sweetness cozies up to a sharp cheddar and aromatic sage, resulting in a dish that's just as exquisite to behold as it is to munch on. I love serving this as an appetizer at autumnal gatherings, sliced into thin wedges. *Makes: 8 to 10 servings*

YOU WILL NEED

½ recipe Basic Pie Dough (page 21)

Large un-rimmed baking sheet

FILLING

1½ pounds butternut squash, peeled, seeded, and cubed

1 medium-size red onion, chopped

1 cup grated sharp cheddar cheese

¼ cup olive oil

2 tablespoons chopped fresh sage or 1 tablespoon dried

1 teaspoon sea salt

Freshly ground black pepper, to taste

EGG WASH

1 large egg yolk

1 tablespoon cold water

Preheat the oven to 375°F.

PREPARE THE CRUST

Remove the chilled pie dough from the refrigerator and roll it out into a 12-inch circle on a lightly floured surface. Transfer the dough to a large un-rimmed baking sheet and refrigerate while you prepare the filling.

PREPARE THE FILLING

Combine all of the filling ingredients in a large bowl.

Using clean hands or a large spoon, toss until well mixed and the squash cubes and onion are well coated with the olive oil and sage.

ASSEMBLE THE TART

Mound the squash mixture in the middle of the chilled pastry circle. Gently spread the mixture out toward the edge of the pastry, leaving a 2-inch border all around.

Fold the pastry border up over the filling, overlapping the edges and pressing the folds together every few inches.

Whisk the egg yolk and water in a small bowl, then use a pastry brush to brush the wash over the folded edges of the crust.

Bake for 40 to 45 minutes, until the crust is golden brown and the squash cubes are tender when pierced with a fork.

Cool the galette at least 30 minutes before serving.

GALUMPKIS PIE

This dish is a pie version of traditional Polish stuffed cabbage rolls. Instead of wrapping up the filling parcel style, I've layered boiled cabbage leaves between a savory meat, rice, herb, and tomato blend, then cradled the whole concoction in a flaky pastry base. The filling calls for ground beef; ground chuck or lamb will both work equally well. This pie is perfect when partnered with a glass of Shiraz or a stout beer. *Makes: 6 to 8 servings*

YOU WILL NEED

- ½ recipe Basic Pie Dough (page 21)
- 9 x 9-inch baking dish

FILLING

- 1 teaspoon sea salt, and more to taste
- 1 medium head cabbage
- 2 tablespoons unsalted butter, melted
- 3 tablespoons olive oil
- 1 medium onion, diced
- 3 cloves garlic, minced
- 2 pounds ground meat
- 1 can (28 ounces) diced tomatoes
- 2 tablespoons granulated sugar
- ½ cup red or white wine
- 3 tablespoons white wine vinegar
- 1 teaspoon lemon juice
- 2 teaspoons chopped fresh thyme or 1 teaspoon dried
- 1 teaspoon chopped fresh dill or ½ teaspoon dried
- ¼ teaspoon ground cloves
- Dash of hot sauce, optional
- Freshly ground black pepper, to taste
- 1 tablespoon all-purpose flour
- 1 cup cooked long-grain rice
- 1 large egg, beaten

EGG WASH

- 1 large egg yolk
- 1 tablespoon cold water

PREPARE THE CRUST

Butter the baking dish and set aside.

Remove the chilled pie dough from the refrigerator and roll it out into a 12-inch circle on a lightly floured surface. Transfer the dough to the prepared baking dish. Press the dough against the bottom and sides and into the corners of the dish. Trim the crust overhang to 1 inch.

Refrigerate while you prepare the filling.

PREPARE THE CABBAGE LEAVES

Fill a large pot with water and the salt. Bring to a boil over high heat while you prep the cabbage head.

Discard the outer leaves, then cut out the core of the cabbage with a sharp knife and carefully remove about half of the leaves.

Cook the cabbage leaves in the boiling salted water 8 to 10 minutes, until limp.

Drain the leaves in a colander, then transfer to a large bowl and toss with the melted butter. Set aside while you preparing the meat filling.

PREPARE THE MEAT FILLING

Heat the olive oil in a large deep skillet saucepan over medium heat. Add the onion and cook for 10 minutes, until fragrant and slightly browned.

Add the garlic and cook 2 to 3 minutes until fragrant, then add the ground meat, stirring until it is well mixed in with the onion and garlic. Cook 5 minutes, stirring occasionally.

Add the tomatoes, sugar, wine, vinegar, lemon juice, thyme, dill, cloves, hot sauce, and salt and pepper to taste.

Cook, uncovered, 30 minutes, stirring occasionally, until the meat is browned.

Stir in the flour and cook 5 minutes, stirring occasionally, until slightly thickened.

Remove from the heat and transfer the meat mixture to a large bowl. Add the rice and stir to fully incorporate, then stir in the beaten egg until well blended.

ASSEMBLE THE PIE

Preheat the oven to 375°F.

Place about one-third of the cabbage leaves on the bottom of the dough-lined baking dish. Spread half the meat mixture on top of that, then layer half of the remaining cabbage leaves on top of the meat mixture.

Add a layer of the remaining meat mixture and top with the remaining cabbage leaves.

Whisk the egg yolk and water in a small bowl, then use a pastry brush to brush the wash over the edges of the crust.

Bake for 30 minutes, until the cabbage leaves are browned and the crust edges are lightly browned.

Cool at least 25 minutes before serving.

TURKEY SHEPHERD'S PIE

When the holiday season rolls around, many of us end up with a fair share of turkey on our hands. After having your fill of turkey sandwiches, turn to this pie solution for creatively using up the remainder. Nestled in a creamy filling of fennel bulb, carrots, celery, and onions, then topped off with buttery mashed potatoes, this potpie is equally at home at a casual get together or a more formal, festive occasion. *Makes: 6 to 8 servings*

YOU WILL NEED

½ recipe Basic Pie Dough (page 21)

9-inch deep-dish pie plate

FILLING

5   tablespoons unsalted butter

2   tablespoons olive oil

½   medium-size onion, diced

2   carrots, peeled and diced

2   celery stalks, trimmed and diced

1   fennel bulb , trimmed and diced

2   cloves garlic, minced

3   tablespoons all-purpose flour

1½ pounds cooked turkey, cut into
    bite-size chunks

1   cup half-and-half

½   cup white wine

2   teaspoons chopped fresh thyme or 1
    teaspoon dried

1   teaspoon chopped fresh sage or ½ teaspoon
    dried

¼   cup chopped fennel fronds

¼   cup chopped carrot top greens or parsley

1   teaspoon sea salt

    Freshly ground black pepper, to taste

MASHED POTATO TOPPING

2   teaspoons sea salt

2   pounds Yukon gold or other medium starch
    potatoes, scrubbed and quartered

¾   cup heavy cream

4   tablespoons (½ stick) unsalted butter, cubed

    Freshly ground black pepper, to taste

1   large egg yolk, beaten, for brushing

PREPARE THE CRUST

Roll out the dough on a lightly floured surface and fit it into the 9-inch deep-dish pie plate. Trim the crust overhang to 1 inch and crimp the edges decoratively. Place the crust in the refrigerator while you prepare the filling.

PREPARE THE FILLING

Heat 2 tablespoons of the butter and the olive oil in a medium-large saucepan over medium heat. Add the onions, carrots, celery, fennel, and garlic. Cook, stirring frequently, for 15 minutes, until the onion is lightly browned and the vegetables are fragrant.

Push the vegetable mixture up against the sides of the pan with a spatula, creating an empty space in the center.

Add the remaining 3 tablespoons butter to the empty space, and when it has melted, whisk in the flour until it turns a blond color.

Stir the vegetables back into the roux, mixing to coat well.

Add the chunks of turkey, half-and-half, wine, thyme, sage, fennel fronds, carrot top greens or parsley, salt, and pepper to the vegetable mixture. Stir until everything is well mixed.

Simmer over medium-low heat 15 minutes, until the mixture thickens. Remove from the heat.

PREPARE THE MASHED POTATO TOPPING

Fill a large pot with water and 1 teaspoon of salt. Bring to a boil over high heat.

Add the potatoes, reduce the heat to medium, and cook 30 minutes.

Drain the potatoes in a colander, removing any big pieces of skin that may have come off while boiling.

Transfer the potatoes to a large bowl and mash, using either a potato masher or a handheld mixer. Add the cream, butter, remaining salt, and pepper. Stir until the butter is melted and all of the ingredients are well incorporated. It's perfectly fine for the mixture to be a bit chunky.

ASSEMBLE THE PIE

Preheat the oven to 375°F.

Fill the prepared crust with the turkey mixture, using a spatula to distribute it evenly. Carefully spoon the mashed potatoes over the turkey mixture.

Brush the crust and the mashed potatoes with the beaten egg yolk, then bake for 45 minutes, until the crust edges are golden and the mashed potato topping is bright yellow.

Cool at least 20 to 25 minutes before serving.

VARIATION: For a meat-free offering, replace the turkey with an equal amount of cooked tempeh.

Kate Payne www.hipgirlshome.com

Kate Payne owns a feather duster and jam jars, and isn't afraid to use them. As the voice behind the blog The Hip Girl's Guide to Homemaking, and author of the book with the same title, she knows a thing or two (or twenty) about keeping house. In both her blog and book, Kate details what she refers to as hip tricks: smart tidbits for being one's best domestic self without breaking the bank. A gluten–free cook, Kate offers here her go–to recipe for a delicious autumn streusel apple pie. It's designed for those sensitive to gluten, but it's sure to please everyone gathered around the table.

GLUTEN-FREE STREUSEL APPLE PIE

Makes: One 9-inch pie

YOU WILL NEED

    Large dinner plate
    9-inch pie pan

CRUST

    1 cup white rice flour
    ¼ cup buckwheat flour
    ¼ cup sweet rice flour
    ½ cup potato starch
    ½ teaspoon xanthan gum
      (Or use 2 cups GF flour mix instead of the
      above ingredients)
    2 teaspoons granulated sugar
    ½ teaspoon salt (I use finely ground sea salt)
    8 tablespoons (1 stick) cold butter, cut into
      ½-inch slices
    1 large egg
    1 tablespoon apple cider vinegar
    4 tablespoons ice water

FILLING

    ½ lemon
    4 medium-size apples, peeled, cored, and
      sliced into ¼-inch slivers
    ½ cup granulated sugar
    ½ teaspoon ground cinnamon
      Pinch of cloves
      Pinch of nutmeg

CRUMB TOPPING

    ¼ cup brown rice flour
    2 tablespoons buckwheat flour
    2 tablespoons potato starch
      Pinch of xanthan gum
      (Or use ½ cup GF flour mix for the above
      ingredients)
    ¼ cup (packed) light brown sugar
    ¼ teaspoon ground cinnamon
      Pinch of salt
      Pinch of nutmeg (optional)
    4 tablespoons (½ stick) unsalted butter

1 large egg, separated, to brush the crust

DAY ONE

MAKE THE DOUGH

Spread two large pieces (at least 18 inches long) of parchment paper out and set aside on a clean work-space.

In a large bowl, mix together the flours, potato starch, and xanthan gum (or use a GF flour mix).

Add the sugar and salt to the flour.

Drop the sliced butter into the dry mix, and use a pastry blender or a fork to incorporate. The mix will still be floury and dry, but the largest butter bits should be about pea-sized.

In a small bowl, whisk together the egg and apple cider vinegar.

Incorporate the egg mixture into the dry crumbles with a fork until all the crumbles are coated (there'll still be lots of dry stuff, just slightly darker-hued).

Add 2 tablespoons of the ice water to the flour mixture and press with your hands to incorporate. It might stick to your hands, but just scrape it off and do your best. Assess the dry/wet situation and add 2 more tablespoons of ice water as needed to finish adhering your dough. You want "stays-together-when-pressed" but not sticky and gooey, nor the other extreme of too dry and crumbly. Dump the now-balled-up dough and any extra crumbles on one sheet of the waiting parchment paper.

Using the heels of your hands, swiftly smash the dough down to form a flat circle. Use your fingers to connect and smooth the cracks that form around the edges of the circle.

Slide the dough disc on its parchment paper onto a dinner plate, and place the top piece of parchment over the dough. Fold the edges of paper to fit on the plate and cover with plastic wrap. Place in the refrigerator overnight, or in the freezer for 1 hour.

DAY TWO

Remove your dough disc from the fridge. Preheat the oven to 400°F.

PREPARE THE FILLING

Squeeze and strain the juice from the lemon into a large bowl. Add the apples.

Add the remaining filling ingredients, combine thoroughly, and set aside.

PREPARE THE CRUMB TOPPING

In a small bowl, mix together the flours, potato starch, and xanthan gum (or use a GF flour mix). Mix in the light brown sugar.

Add the cinnamon, salt, and nutmeg to the flour.

Melt the butter and pour it over the dry ingredients. Use a fork to incorporate the butter and crumble up the mixture.

PREPARE THE CRUST

Roll out the dough, keeping the parchment lining on both sides. It might crack along the edges as you roll from the center into a wider and flatter circle. Take your pin and roll along the edges of your circle, clockwise, to help close those cracks (use your fingers if need be). Roll to a 13-inch diameter.

Slide a cutting board or cookie sheet under your rolled out parchment-sandwiched circle, remove the top sheet of parchment, and gently place your 9-inch pie pan upside down on the dough. Holding everything over the counter, make a swift, confident flip of your pan and cookie sheet to droop the crust into the pan. Remove the last piece of parchment paper and assist the dough in sagging down snugly in the pie pan. Don't worry if the edges crumble off. Just reattach them as you flute or crimp the edge of the crust.

ASSEMBLE THE PIE

Brush the unbaked crust with an egg yolk (or an egg white; I like the golden color of the yolk, but it's up to you).

Add the apples, using a spatula to evenly distribute them in the pan.

Spread the streusel crumbles on top of the apples.

Bake for 30 minutes, then rotate the pie and cover it with a piece of aluminum foil if the top is browning too fast. Bake for another 20 minutes, or until the apples bubble up through the crumbs.

Allow to cool completely before serving.

Jenna Woginrich www.coldantlerfarm.com

Jenna walks a daily tightrope, performing a balancing act between life as a full-time graphic designer with that of caretaker to the menagerie of animals on her six-acre New York homestead. She blogs about her triumphs and travails at Cold Antler Farm and has written a book, *Made From Scratch*, about her journey as a young single woman homesteading in Idaho and Vermont while holding down a career off the farm. She's also penned a book on caring for baby chicks, *Chick Days*, and has a new book, *Barnheart: The Incurable Longing for a Farm of One's Own*. Here she's sharing her recipe for an autumn harvest quiche, inspired by the butchering of a hog she raised (she provides nonmeat substitutes for vegetarian readers, as well).

HARVEST QUICHE

Makes: One 9-inch pie

YOU WILL NEED

½ recipe Basic Pie Dough (page 21)
   9-inch pie pan

FILLING

 2 broccoli crowns
   Salt
 2 tablespoons olive oil
⅓ cup diced onion
 7 large eggs
 1 cup half-and-half
 4 to 6 slices bacon, cooked and chopped, or 8 ounces sausage, cooked and crumbled
1½ cups shredded cheddar and/or Monterey Jack cheese
   Freshly ground black pepper, to taste

Preheat the oven to 350°F.

PREPARE THE CRUST

Roll out the dough on a lightly floured surface and fit it into the 9-inch pie pan. Trim the crust overhang to 1 inch and crimp the edges decoratively. Place the crust in the refrigerator while you prepare the filling.

PREPARE THE FILLING

Cut the broccoli into 1-inch pieces and steam them, sprinkling with a few shakes of salt as you do so. Drain the broccoli and set aside.

Heat the olive oil in a small skillet. Add the onion and caramelize, stirring, over medium heat. Remove from the heat and set aside.

In a medium-size bowl, quickly beat the eggs and half-and-half together into a uniform yellow liquid. Set aside.

ASSEMBLE THE QUICHE

Scatter the caramelized onions over the bottom of the piecrust. Place the cooked broccoli crowns on top, then scatter your precooked meats throughout.

Take a handful of shredded cheese and cover your meat and vegetables, creating a mid-layer of cheese for the pie.

Pour over the egg mixture, filling in the entire pie but leaving at least a inch of space at the top of the crust.

Cover the filling with another handful of cheese, and sprinkle with a hearty spicing of pepper.

Bake for about 45 to 50 minutes, or until the top is lightly browned and a knife comes out clean, with no runny egg on it.

VARIATION: For a vegetarian version, simply omit the real meats and replace with imitation, which actually taste pretty darn good in there.

RESOURCES

INGREDIENTS

ARROWROOT POWDER

Frontier
www.frontiercoop.com

Mountain Rose Herbs
www.mountainroseherbs.com

CULTURED BUTTER

Organic Valley
www.organicvalley.coop

Vermont Cultured Butter
www.vermontcreamery.com

FAIR-TRADE CHOCOLATE

Dagoba
www.dagobachocolate.com

Divine
www.divinechocolate.com

Green & Black's
www.greenandblacks.com

Theo
www.theochocolate.com

FLAVOR EXTRACTS

Simply Organic
www.simplyorganicfoods.com

HAZELNUT FLOUR

Bob's Red Mill
www. bobsredmill.com

POTATO FLOUR

Ener-G Foods
www.ener-g.com

SPICES

Frontier
www.frontiercoop.com

The Spice Hunter
www.spicehunter.com

SHORTENING

Spectrum
www.spectrumorganics.com

TAPIOCA STARCH

King Arthur Flour
www.kingarthurflour.com

EQUIPMENT

PASTRY CUTTER

Cuisipro
www.cuisipro.com

Oxo
www.oxo.com

PIE PANS

The Pampered Chef
www.pamperedchef.com

Sur La Table
www.surlatable.com

Williams-Sonoma
www.williams-sonoma.com

PIE WEIGHTS

Fox Run
www.foxrunbrands.com

ROLLING PINS

Oxo
www.oxo.com

SILICONE BAKING MATS

Silpat
www.silpat.com

TART AND SPRINGFORM PANS

Calphalon
www.calphalon.com

Chicago Metallic
www.chicago-metallic.com

Nordic Ware
www.nordicware.com

METRIC CONVERSION CHART BY VOLUME
(for Liquids)

U.S.	Metric (milliliters/liters)
$\frac{1}{4}$ teaspoon	1.25 mL
$\frac{1}{2}$ teaspoon	2.5 mL
1 teaspoon	5 mL
1 tablespoon	15 mL
$\frac{1}{4}$ cup	60 mL
$\frac{1}{2}$ cup	120 mL
$\frac{3}{4}$ cup	180 mL
1 cup	240 mL
2 cups (1 pint)	480 mL
4 cups (1 quart)	960 mL
4 quarts (1 gallon)	3.8 L

METRIC CONVERSION CHART BY WEIGHT
(for Dry Ingredients)

U.S.	Metric (grams/kilograms)
$\frac{1}{4}$ teaspoon	1 g
$\frac{1}{2}$ teaspoon	2 g
1 teaspoon	5 g
1 tablespoon	15 g
16 ounces (1 pound)	450 g
2 pounds	900 g
3 pounds	1.4 kg
4 pounds	1.8 kg
5 pounds	2.3 kg
6 pounds	2.7 kg

COOKING MEASUREMENT EQUIVALENTS

3 teaspoons = 1 tablespoon

2 tablespoons = 1 fluid ounce

4 tablespoons = $\frac{1}{4}$ cup

5 tablespoons + 1 teaspoon = $\frac{1}{3}$ cup

8 tablespoons = $\frac{1}{2}$ cup

10 tablespoons + 2 teaspoons = $\frac{2}{3}$ cup

12 tablespoons = $\frac{3}{4}$ cup

16 tablespoons = 1 cup

48 teaspoons = 1 cup

1 cup = 8 fluid ounces

2 cups = 1 pint

2 pints = 1 quart

4 quarts = 1 gallon

TEMPERATURE CONVERSION

Fahrenheit	Celsius
32°	0°
212°	100°
250°	121°
275°	135°
300°	149°
350°	177°
375°	191°
400°	204°
425°	218°

ACKNOWLEDGMENTS

Everything wonderful in life occurs when delighted by the company of others, I've long believed. As such, this book owes so very much to the efforts of a smattering of wonderful people.

To the inspiring and accommodating recipe contributors: Aran Goyoaga, Tricia Martin, Tim Mazurek, Jessie Oleson, Kate Payne, Beatrice Peltre, Amanda Soule, and Jenna Woginrich. Thank you all for your tantalizingly sweet and savory additions to this book, and for your willingness to join me in this perennial pie-making journey.

Photographer Lynne Harty always captures just the right shot every time. This is our fifth collaboration and I absolutely adore working with her. Art Directors Travis Medford and Kristi Pfeffer deserve profuse praise for their beautiful designs, layout, and genius ability to make pie magic happen on paper.

Abundant thanks are offered to Chris Bryant and Skip Wade for opening up their home to numerous pie shoots, allowing us to spill flour and butter crumbs on their countertops without complaint. A river of gratitude also goes out to Chris for his expert artistic eye and ability to make food look as delectable and beautiful as imaginable.

Heartfelt thanks to Nicole McConville and Beth Sweet, for presenting me with such a fun and "sweet" opportunity. Working with you ladies as co-editors is the best case scenario a writer could ever hope for.

For my husband Glenn, I can't thank you enough for your extraordinary encouragement and generosity. Your insight into flavorful combinations, sage and seasoned palate, and willingness to eat pie for 6 months straight helped save many a pie and my sanity. You are my co-conspirator in all things great and small. I love you so very, very much.

Finally, special thanks to my in-laws, Clifford and Barbara English, and to my parents, Jim and Diane. Your tips, suggestions, and rousing conversations provided me with an arsenal of pie-baking ideas.

ABOUT THE AUTHOR

Ashley English has degrees in both holistic nutrition and sociology. She has worked with numerous non-profit organizations committed to social and agricultural issues, is a member of Slow Food USA, and has had a regular column for the popular blog Design*Sponge. Ashley and her family live in Candler, NC, with their menagerie of chickens, dogs, cats, and bees, where they are converting their land into a thriving homestead. Follow her tales of living a homemade life at www.small-measure.blogspot.com.

ALSO AVAILABLE FROM ASHLEY ENGLISH